Unresolved Grief and Loss

To Maggie
Thanks for your support.
Dr Moss-King

Davina Moss-King

Unresolved Grief and Loss Issues Related to Heroin Recovery

Grief and Loss with Heroin Recovery

VDM Verlag Dr. Müller

Impressum/Imprint (nur für Deutschland/ only for Germany)
Bibliografische Information der Deutschen Nationalbibliothek: Die Deutsche Nationalbibliothek verzeichnet diese Publikation in der Deutschen Nationalbibliografie; detaillierte bibliografische Daten sind im Internet über http://dnb.d-nb.de abrufbar.

Coverbild: www.purestockx.com

Verlag: VDM Verlag Dr. Müller Aktiengesellschaft & Co. KG
Dudweiler Landstr. 99, 66123 Saarbrücken, Deutschland
Telefon +49 681 9100-698, Telefax +49 681 9100-988, Email: info@vdm-verlag.de
Zugl.: Buffalo, State University of New York at Buffalo, Diss., 2005

Herstellung in Deutschland:
Schaltungsdienst Lange o.H.G., Berlin
Books on Demand GmbH, Norderstedt
Reha GmbH, Saarbrücken
Amazon Distribution GmbH, Leipzig
ISBN: 978-3-639-16653-8

Imprint (only for USA, GB)
Bibliographic information published by the Deutsche Nationalbibliothek: The Deutsche Nationalbibliothek lists this publication in the Deutsche Nationalbibliografie; detailed bibliographic data are available in the Internet at http://dnb.d-nb.de.

Cover image: www.purestockx.com

Publisher:
VDM Verlag Dr. Müller Aktiengesellschaft & Co. KG
Dudweiler Landstr. 99, 66123 Saarbrücken, Germany
Phone +49 681 9100-698, Fax +49 681 9100-988, Email: info@vdm-publishing.com
Buffalo, State University of New York at Buffalo, Diss., 2005

Printed in the U.S.A.
Printed in the U.K. by (see last page)
ISBN: 978-3-639-16653-8

Acknowledgments

This book is dedicated to the individuals recovering from heroin addiction and the therapists that assist in the healing process. I would like to give my thanks to my loving husband Darryl, my daughter Nia and my unborn "baby King" along with my parents and three step-children.

TABLE OF CONTENTS

APPENDICES

Abstract

Research has shown that heroin addicts have low recovery rates following detoxification and have a high treatment recidivism rate. The heroin addicts will usually relapse at least 72 hours following discharge from treatment and these addicts do not have appropriate coping skills to prevent a relapse.

There has been research that compares the loss of substances similar to a death or a grief and loss issue. The past research does not address the relationship that the addict has with the heroin. This study, however, examined the losses related to the heroin use that the addict experienced due to ending the relationship with the drug. The qualitative research method of grounded theory for data collection and analysis was used. The principal investigator interviewed 12 heroin addicts in a detoxification facility one time each discussing the losses related to the addiction and the grief the addicts experienced while in treatment.

The analysis indicated that the recovering heroin addicts grieve the **loss of the heroin**, **heroin culture**, and **heroin lifestyle** and **lack coping skills and desire to address these areas in treatment**. This analysis also revealed that the recovering heroin addict has difficulty ending their relationship with the drug and this result is unresolved grief that may lead to chronic relapses.

The results of the study add to the addiction literature because it takes an in-depth examination of the emotional attachment to heroin and its counterparts as well as revealing the lack of coping skills that the recovering addict has to resolve the grieving issues related to the heroin.

CHAPTER I
INTRODUCTION

Personal Statement

I have worked in the field of chemical dependency for eighteen years; eight of the eighteen years I have counseled individuals with opiate dependence. While working with this population I have observed a reoccurrence of detoxification and rehabilitation at the inpatient level. During the intake process, it is common practice to inquire about the recent relapse or the chief complaint that has resulted in an inpatient detoxification or rehabilitation stay. The clientele typically respond to this inquiry by stating they had difficulty developing new coping skills as well as new relationships. The clientele find it easy to develop new relationships while in active addiction; however, lack confidence in relationships when not using the opiate (heroin). These individuals often state that their continuous struggle is to be "normal" in society. The clientele attribute their failure to lead a "normal" life to their inability to detach from the drug lifestyle as well as to depend on the heroin to assist with coping during difficult life situations. Some difficult situations include loss of a loved one and loss of the drug culture. As a result, the individual addicted to heroin needs to develop appropriate strategies during the rehabilitation phase to have a successful recovery.

During my eight years as a clinician and assisting the clients in the recovery process, I have discovered that the clients grieve the loss of the heroin very much the same as a human grieves a loved one. There are some clients who compare the early recovery process to facing a death. The clients often claim during individual or group sessions that their life will never be the same and there is uncertainty of functioning without the heroin.

As a result of listening, counseling, and attempting to understand the heroin recovery process that seems to surround grief and loss issues, this project was developed.

Heroin Epidemic

There has been an epidemic of heroin use since the 1800's. Heroin is known as the semi synthetic of natural opioid such as morphine. Prior to the creation of heroin most individuals were using morphine for medical purposes and for enjoyment. Hippocrates used morphine for treating internal diseases, diseases of women and various epidemics. Heroin itself was not created until 1874 by an English researcher, C. R. Wright who decided to boil morphine on his stove and use the contents intravenously. This researcher then proclaimed that heroin could be used to help any individual detoxify or to reduce their morphine addiction. This information spread through out the medical world and during the beginning of the 1900's the St. James society mailed free samples of heroin to morphine addicts. The morphine epidemic soon became reversed to the heroin epidemic. Individuals that were addicted to morphine were now addicted to heroin. The heroin epidemic became widely known in major metropolitan cities such as New York where individuals were often buying the drug from the streets and using in their homes for enjoyment. As a result in 1923 the U. S. Treasury Department's Narcotics Division (the first federal drug agency) banned all legal narcotic sales along with the prohibition of legal venues to purchase heroin, addicts were forced to buy from illegal street dealers (Frontline, 1999 p. 6). Since 1923 there have been heroin sales from the streets not only in New York City, but also in other metropolitan and small cities alike.

Thereafter there have been laws attempting to bring the heroin epidemic under control. The District of Columbia Pharmacy Act of 1906 was in the interest of physicians and pharmacists to prescribe minimum amounts of opium or the derivatives of opium, in particular heroin in patent medicines. These medications could be re-prescribed by the physician if he / she believed that the re-prescription was necessary for a cure of the illness (Platt, 1986). The Pure Food and Drug Act of 1906 required the listing of the opium on all medications that were patented (Platt, 1986). The Harrison Act of 1914 "made dispensing of narcotic drugs unlawful except by physicians for legitimate medical purposes" (Platt, 1986 p. 18). In the Jin Fuey decision of 1915 was from the court case the United States v. Jin Fuey Moy (1915). The Supreme Court heard the case regarding the physician Dr. Moy who prescribed 1/16 ounce of a narcotic to an individual that was addicted to opium. The government expressed to Dr. Moy that he violated the Harrison Act of 1914. The government assumed that Dr. Moy was attempting to maintain the individual's opium habit by prescribing the narcotic. The result of this case was that it was unconstitutional for the government to intervene with the physician's practice of medicine. This court case and its decision impaired the power of Congress to enforce the Harrison Act of 1914 (Platt, 1986).

However, in 1920 the Supreme Court ruled against Dr. Moy and stated that a physician cannot supply or prescribe a narcotic to an addict to assist patients in their addiction or to maintain their addiction (Platt, 1986). This decision came immediately following the Webb and Doremus Decisions of 1919. These decisions came from two cases United States v. Doremus

(1919) and Webb et al. v. United States (1919). The Doremus case involved Dr. Charles Doremus prescribing 500 1/6 ounce morphine tablets to maintain the opium habit of an addict. The Webb et al. v. United States the Supreme Court ruled that prescribing narcotics to an individual to maintain an opium habit was illegal. In these two cases the Supreme Court ruled that each violated the Harrison Act of 1914 (Platt, 1986). As a result of these two cases, many physicians in New York City were arrested for supplying narcotics to maintain the habit of those addicted.

Throughout the history of narcotics, drugs have been exported and imported from various parts of the world. Following the Supreme Court rulings, Congress needed to intervene to restrict the import and export of opium. As a result the intervention included the Jones-Miller Act of 1922 or the Narcotic Drugs and Export Act of 1922 (Platt, 1986).

The Jones-Miller Act of 1922 proposed legislation in 1924 to ban the domestic manufacture of heroin. There were several testimonies before the Supreme Court stating that heroin was highly addictive and that there was a correlation between high crime and continued use of heroin. This legislation created the assumption, that heroin addiction was a disease and needed to be treated as such. Following this assumption the Linder Decision of 1925 enforced the thought that heroin addiction was a disease. The case of Linder v. United States of 1925 stated that Dr. Linder had given a female addict a prescribed narcotic to alleviate symptoms of withdrawal from her addiction to heroin. As a result of this Supreme Court decision there was a conflict with the Harrison Act of 1914 regarding prescribing narcotics in good faith according to the physician's medical judgment.

These acts and court cases illustrate the evolution of heroin use. Increased heroin use created urgency for medical care to assist the addict to withdraw safely from heroin. As a result, hospitals in Lexington, Kentucky in 1935 and in Fort Worth, Texas in 1938 were the first two institutions with programs that specialized in heroin addiction withdrawal and rehabilitation. The Public Health Service, under the direction of the Justice Department and the Federal Bureau of Narcotics, monitored the two hospitals (Platt, 1986). These two hospitals' rehabilitation and detoxification models are still used today for the inpatient and outpatient rehabilitation recovery for a heroin addict. All of these acts mentioned above led the way to the Narcotic Addict Rehabilitation Act of 1966 which provided inpatient and outpatient treatment for heroin addicts.

The Comprehensive Drug Abuse Prevention and Control Act of 1970 created schedules (levels) for the potential of drug abuse. Narcotics are at schedule one, which states that it is highly addictive and that a person faces the maximum penalties if caught with the possession of heroin or any narcotic. The Narcotic Addict Treatment Act NATA of 1974 was designed by the Department of Health and Human Services to establish standards for the use by practitioners of narcotic drugs for maintenance or detoxification of narcotic-addicted persons. Actual regulation of narcotic treatment programs under NATA was delegated to the Food and Drug Administration (Platt, 1986).

The Substance Abuse and Mental Health Services Administration (SAMHSA), an agency of the United States Department of Health and Human Services, submits for publication each year the Treatment Episode Data Set (TEDS) that includes the number of individuals that received substance abuse treatment by demographics and by the substance. According to TEDS, heroin was the most common drug among inpatient treatment admissions during the year of 2000 - 11% of 1.6 million substance abuse admissions) and in the year of 2002 - 15% of 1.9 million admissions). There was an increase of individuals receiving treatment for heroin use, in the year 2000 - 273,446; in 2001- 277,911 and during the year 2002 - 285,667 individuals were treated for heroin use. There were also individuals treated for opiates other than heroin, 2000 -29,054, 2001 - 38,462 and 2002 - 45,605 (Treatment Episode Data Set, 2004).

Physical Effects of Heroin

Opioids enter the body intravenously, intramuscularly, or via nasal mucosa or the lungs. Once in the bloodstream, the substance is distributed throughout the body. The substance then lands in the brain, kidney, lung, liver, spleen, digestive tract, and muscle. Once the opiate binds with the mu receptors it binds with the liver to attempt to detoxify. The body naturally has the detoxifying agent called glucuronic acid. The glucuronic acid is already formed in the liver prepared to detoxify opiates. Its function is to take the poisonous substances to be more water-soluble and then to be excreted via the kidneys (Schuster & Kuhar, 1996).

The use of heroin chronically affects the stomach and the small intestine along with the large intestine as a result greater amount of water is absorbed in the gastrointestinal tract of the human (Schuster & Kuhar, 1996). The extra water is absorbed in the gastrointestinal tract, which results in constipation (Howard, 2003).

Individuals addicted to heroin have a reduction in the T-Cells because of constant break down of the endocrine system that is also responsible for the immune system (Schuster & Kuhar, 1996). The T-cells are developed in the thymus and are responsible for destroying infected cells. The chronic use of heroin, however, causes infection of the heart valves and the lining of the heart valves. Chronic use of heroin intravenously can produce collapsed veins and arthritis for repeatedly using the syringe in the same area (Howard, 2003).

Individuals who use heroin for the first time usually report a rush feeling of pleasurable sensations. The rush feeling is normally accompanied by a warm feeling on the skin. The user will admit to having a dry mouth and the sensations that the arms and legs are very heavy. Upon the administration effects are felt within 10 to 15 minutes if taken nasal mucous or via lungs; seven to eight seconds if administered intravenously. Soon after the seconds or minutes have passed after using the heroin, the individual will experience nausea, vomiting and severe itching. After the initial affects the individual will experience slowed breathing, along with slowed cardiac functioning. If the breathing is depressed for a length of time, the individual could possibly reach the point of death or a coma (Platt, 1986).

The individual who chooses to use heroin recreationally often discovers that he or she is addicted. An individual usually becomes addicted after a few weeks of continued use. Withdraw symptoms usually begin within a few hours of the last use. Withdraw symptoms are resembling flu-like symptoms: runny nose, abdominal cramps, diarrhea, muscle and bone pain, vomiting, and cold flashes with goose bumps along with involuntary leg movements. Heroin users administer the drug many times throughout the day to avoid these withdrawal symptoms that are not fatal, but an individual that is having such symptoms should be advised to seek medical attention. The symptoms are able to last between 24 to 48 hours; the first 72 hours are so critical that one should seek medical attention while going through the physical withdrawal. The heroin addict begins to experience withdrawal symptoms when:

> The brain senses an overabundance of what it thinks are endorphins, and attempts to restore balance itself by shutting down its own production of real endorphins. It continues to do so whether or not the addict is currently high on heroin. The addict's body must therefore depend entirely on heroin to regulate various bodily functions that are no longer regulated by endorphins. When there is no heroin present, these functions

cease to operate properly thereby triggering the wide variety of symptoms associated with withdrawal. (Howard, 2003, p. 48)

The heroin addict's body also has a way of regulating withdrawal by creating tolerance. As the heroin addict uses steadily overtime there is a need to use more heroin to obtain homeostasis in the brain (Platt, 1986).

Long – term effects of heroin use

An individual that has been a chronic user of heroin for many years will begin to notice some physical changes. The addict will begin to notice drooping of the eyelids, constricted pupils, slurred speech, a raspy voice for males and females, very dry skin and constant constipation. As mentioned earlier, the hormone levels are decreased with continued use. As a result of the hormone levels decreasing the addict will begin to have problems with his or her health. One of the main health issues is Human Immunodeficiency Virus (H.I.V.) because of the decrease of t-cells and the lack of hormones from the endocrine system. Since the addict's immune system is not functioning properly, the addict will have non-contagious infections that I.V. drug users will experience. Some of these skin infections are at the site of the injection which results in skin ulcers, abscesses and fungal infections will occur.

Psychological long – term effects

Since the addict has become solely dependent on the heroin to handle life situations, he or she will be less able to cope with any situations without the use of heroin (Howard, 2003)

The individual that has become addicted to heroin will experience physical withdrawal. Along with the physical withdrawal the individual will experience depression and acute anxiety (Howard, 2003). Howard (2003) also states that the addict's emotional development is halted at the time of use. Therefore while in treatment the heroin addict could behave immaturely.

As the individual becomes more interested in the drug he or she may become less interested in friends and family. The individual gravitates toward individuals that are sharing in the obsession of using heroin. Soon the addict develops antisocial behavior and becomes de-sensitized to society's rules. As a result, the addict might commit crimes and do other things to obtain the drug. These crimes are usually done out of desperation to not experience the withdrawal symptoms.

Emotional Issues Related to Substance Abuse

Individuals attempting to recover from heroin addiction through treatment may experience emotions related to the heroin use. There are individuals that experience depression while in detoxification treatment or during the rehabilitation phase of treatment. There is literature that supports the relationship between addiction and depression. Depressive symptomatology presents itself during the beginning phases of treatment when the opiate addict is in withdrawal. There is a desire to obtain the drug to relieve withdrawal symptoms are the catalyst of the individual's symptomatology. Along with a desire to use the drug, the addict may experience grief that is associated with the loss of the heroin to relieve the discomfort. The loss of the heroin plays a vital part in the grieving process during early recovery. Researchers note that heroin addicts become dependent upon the drug for daily functioning and as a coping mechanism. The individual needs to learn new coping skills and to restructure the life he or she knew as an addict.

Depression

The individual recovering from heroin addiction typically suffers from depression during detoxification in which the self-esteem is low and the individual is affected from losing various attachments that occurred during and prior to the addition.

Researchers observe a relationship between addiction and depression. Kosten, Rounsaville and Kleber (1983) studied recent life events and stressors six months after detoxification treatment. Of the 123 participants in the study, 45% were diagnosed with depression while in the inpatient facility and six months after discharge the participants continued to be depressed. Another 36% of the participants were in remission from depression after being diagnosed at the facility, and 19% did not have symptoms of depression during the six-month follow-up nor while in the inpatient facility for detoxification. This study illustrated that real life situations had a negative effect on the mental health and induced depressive symptoms.

Dai and Zhao (2001) studied the mental health status of individuals addicted to heroin. The results were consistent with previous literature: the subjects scored above the norm scores on depression, anxiety and paranoia. Huang, Wu, Lin, Wen & Zheng (2001) also studied the mental health state of heroin addicts following detoxification and their results were consistent with those of Dai and Zhao. Huang, Wu, Lin, Wen & Zheng's findings state that the heroin addict had severe stressors that led to psychological problems following detoxification that warranted extensive counseling following detoxification treatment.

Grief in Recovery

Some researchers state that depression can be misdiagnosed as actual grief. The symptoms of grief and depression are similar in the physical and emotional effects such as loss of appetite and lack of sleep along with intense sadness. The difference between grief and depression is that for an individual that is depressed he or she may have lower self-esteem, whereas with grief an individual will usually continue to have an average self esteem (Worden, 2002). The individual recovering from heroin addiction suffers from depression during detoxification in which the self-esteem is low and the individual is affected from losing various attachments that occurred during and prior to addiction. However, once the individual has been discharged from treatment the self-esteem is elevated due to a positive environment and constant encouragement during the inpatient rehabilitation phase. The individual may begin to experience the grieving stages of addiction during the recovery phase (McDonald, 1985).

Kubler-Ross (1969) described five stages of grief: denial, anger, sorrow / despair / depression, bargaining, and acceptance. McDonald (1985) used the five stages to explain the grief issues regarding recovery from alcohol addiction. According to McDonald the denial stage is related to an individual denying the destructiveness of alcohol use on self as well as others associated with the individual. The anger stage relates to the individual being angry at himself/ herself for allowing alcohol to consume his / her everyday life and cause destruction in the family system. Sorrow / despair / depression are the result of the individual losing his / her drug of choice. Most often therapists may hear a client stating, "The bottle was my best friend" (McDonald, 1985, p. 8). The result of these feelings leads to catharsis during counseling sessions. The bargaining stage is the recovering alcoholic's attempt to continue to control his / her life with the use of alcohol. This period is usually when the individual attempts to "cut down" the use of alcohol in an attempt to bargain with family members. The stage of acceptance is the final stage of the grieving process in which the individual accepts that he / she is powerless over alcohol and reflects upon the destructive behavior that resulted from alcohol use.

Losses

McGovern (1986) observes that the individual that is recovering from alcoholism has experienced various losses while in active addition. McGovern's study identified some of the losses as follows: the loss of ability to drink normally and to maintain responsible behavior, the loss of ability to regain sobriety, the loss of ability to achieve a euphoric state and the loss of health, the loss of employment, the loss of positive social contacts and the loss of family. According to McGovern when an individual recognizes the losses, he or she can begin recovery in a positive manner.

Along with the above losses, the individual addicted to heroin has a loss of the drug lifestyle. The drug lifestyle can be defined as the individual failing to take responsibility for life's circumstances and to cope effectively without the use of alcohol or drugs. "Stress – coping imbalance occurs as a result of the lifestyle drug abusers' habitual manner of stress management, in which drugs become the primary means of dealing with problems" (Walters, 1994, p. 2). Since habits and rituals of the addictive lifestyle are forming, the individual abandons all positive relationships and bonds even more with the persons with whom he or she is using drugs and alcohol on a daily basis. Along with the lifestyle of coping mechanism there is an involvement with the legal system that becomes part of the lifestyle. According to Platt (1995), the individual addicted to heroin may eventually increase criminal activity as a tolerance for heroin also increases. Merrill, Alterman, Cacciola and Rutherford (1999) argued that individuals in treatment for heroin for at least six or more detox episodes were less likely to be arrested. They concluded that treatment lowers the recidivism rate for criminal activity.

Culture

There is an intriguing and mysterious culture associated with heroin use. One of the cultural events is the use of needles for an immediate high and the injections usually begin in the forearm and gradually become evident in other parts of the body such as the neck and legs (Platt, 1995). There is also in the drug culture of a universal language used by individuals addicted to heroin to relate to each other, excluding non-heroin users from conversations. Most importantly, the individual addicted to heroin has a pleasurable and emotional fixation, which promotes a chemical love that is difficult for the addict to detach from during the recovery period (Platt, 1995).

Premise of the study

This study is based on the assumption that the individual who is attempting to recover from heroin dependency may be grieving the loss of the addict's lifestyle, as well as the loss of the drug itself. The individual has become attached to heroin physically and psychologically.

As a result, the individual needs to be allowed to openly grieve the attachment to the loss of the drug while in an inpatient phase of treatment.

Purpose of the study

The purpose of this study is to provide a framework that therapists and /or clinicians may use when counseling individuals with heroin addiction in an inpatient setting. In this study I examine the grief and loss issues surrounding individuals attempting to recover from heroin addiction and will explore the extent to which patients must first fully grieve their attachments to addiction in order to begin the path of recovery.

Importance or value of the study (what will be known or changed as a result of the study)

The therapist must understand that extracting the drug from the individual's life can be traumatizing. Heroin was used as a coping mechanism especially during successes, disappointments, and difficulties. The patient has come to rely on the drug as one would rely on a best friend or a spouse. As a result of the client being involved with inpatient treatment, the drug is not part of the individual's life, and therefore new coping skills and strategies are necessary (Gossop, Stewart, Brown & Marsden, 2002). This study is important since it is attempting to add an additional way for therapists to assist the patient to develop recovery skills.

The important piece that is missing from inpatient rehabilitation in the area of heroin addiction is that thirty days of rehabilitation is not enough time for an individual to change identity from an addict to a recovering addict (Krueger, 1981). The individual must actually recognize the attachments that resulted from the addiction such as lifestyle, culture, and acquaintances. It is important that the therapist realize that the addict did not obtain these attachments overnight and will not detach from them within thirty days. This detachment is actually a process of grief that usually takes months, and sometimes longer.

The first intent of the study is to enhance the thinking of therapists in the area of grief in heroin addiction recovery. The second intent is to encourage therapists to allow the patients to openly grieve the losses and reduce the disenfranchised grief during the rehabilitation phase.

Rationale and Conceptual Framework (Philosophical / Theoretical perspective)

The rationale of this study comes from the theory of disenfranchised grief (Doka, 1989) and Bowlby's (1969) attachment theory. These two theories are related to the philosophy that individuals must detach themselves from their drug of choice and all aspects of the addiction to enhance sobriety and to be productive members of society.

Disenfranchised Grief

According to Doka (1989) disenfranchised grief is defined as "the grief that a person or persons experience when they incur a loss that is not or cannot be openly acknowledged, publicly mourned or socially supported" (p. 3). The nature of disenfranchised grief is separated into three parts: 1) the relationship is not recognized, 2) the loss is not recognized , and 3) the griever is not recognized.

Relationship

Even in the 21st century where there has been liberation in the area of homosexuality and cohabitation; romantic relationships among gay people are not usually recognized making it difficult for a mate to make end of life decisions for his / her partner. There are other relationships that are not recognized such as an extra marital affair, where the individual would not be allowed to attend the funeral or even be given condolences for the death of the lover. Other relationships involving divorced spouses, stepparents, and in-laws where the griever's relationship is not recognized as a significant and the griever will experience emotional isolation and not be comforted by others. Although the griever's relationship is not readily recognized by society, the griever still mourns the relationship and the past emotions. These losses complicate grief even more for the griever because he / she are not allowed to fully show emotion. This intensifies the emotional feelings of grief, and the individual will frequently experience shame, guilt sadness or depression during the mourning period (Doka, 1989).

Loss

There are other instances where the loss is not recognized as significant and this causes grievers to not share their emotions with others because of shameful feelings or fear that someone will misunderstand. An example of a loss that can be perinatal loss that can be disenfranchised grief. Hazen (2003) argued that mothers that had a miscarriage may suffer from shame and guilt; however, these women may not openly discuss their shame and guilt and this resulted in disenfranchised grief.

Griever

There are certain beliefs in society where the griever is not recognized. There are instances where the individual that has a developmental disability or an emotional disability is thought not to grieve. As a result disabled persons will not be placed in an environment where they are free to grieve; the mourner is not recognized as grieving and, thus she / he experiences disenfranchised grief (Doka, 1989).

Self – disenfranchisement

Self – disenfranchised grief is the individual's lack of acknowledgment of a loss and the recognition of the mourning process within himself / herself. During self – disenfranchisement the individual suffers from shame and guilt for not accepting a loss and these feelings impede and complicate the grieving process. While the individual is experiencing complicated grief he / she may feel out of control, helpless, and lonely that may increase the level of shamefulness (Doka, 1989).

Disenfranchised grief and heroin addiction

Individuals recovering from heroin addiction often experience disenfranchised grief over losing their drug of choice. Recovering addicts have developed friendships and bonds during their addiction. The individual not only became physically dependent, but also became psychologically dependent on heroin. Although, the recovering addict has made a decision to discontinue using drugs and / or alcohol eventually he or she begins to miss the drug with which he / she has developed a bond as well as the relationships found while using it.

One aspect of disenfranchised grief is that the relationship with the heroin is not recognized by society. The result of this phenomenon is shame. An individual recovering from heroin addiction will often experience shameful emotions regarding his / her addiction that may eventually lead to guilt (McDonald, 1985). The philosophy of society is that the individual ought to rejoice when losing the drug of choice as well as the bonding relationships from addiction. However, some of the individuals pursuing recovery have had these relationships from addiction and find it very difficult to start over, as a result, the individual misses the relationships that accompanied the addiction and this conflicts with society's philosophy.

Since society does not look upon drug abuse favorably, recovering addicts seldom reveal their loss of the drug culture or of the bonds that developed via addiction to a therapist, to others and even to themselves. The result of the individual not being able to openly discuss his / her experience regarding the drug of choice and the relationships that accompanied addiction is disenfranchised grief. Once the individual begins to emphatically miss the bond of the drug or of relationships, the recovering addict will often attempt to revisit old friends and these visitations may lead to relapse. When this relationship is rekindled, and guilt along with self-disappointment sets in, the addict may not openly discuss the bond or the attachment.

Attachment Theory

Attachment theory by Bowlby (1969) was developed from the observation of mother and child separation. The physical attachment between an infant and the mother or caregiver is related to the behaviors such as touching and holding. The psychological attachment is related to the emotions created by the relationship between the caregiver and the infant. The love of the caregiver helps the infant feel safe and secure (Sroufe, 1996).

Bowlby (1969) originally developed the attachment theory from observing interaction between infants and mothers or caregivers. Through continuous research, Bowlby saw the attachment between the infant and the mother or caregiver as actually forming a relationship. As a result of forming this relationship, the infant flourishes throughout both childhood and adult life stages.

Attachment behavior results from a person attaining or continuing closeness to a preferred individual. During the development of attachment an affectional bond is made. Initially this bond is developed between child and parent; later the behavior extends to an adult-to-adult relationship (Bowlby, 1980). One of the premises of attachment theory is that the individual strives to maintain the relationship by means of communication or proximity. According to Bowlby many intense emotions are developed during the attachment process and the maintenance of attachment:

> The formation of a bond is described as falling in love, maintaining a bond as loving someone, and losing a partner as grieving over someone. Similarly, the threat of loss arouses anxiety and actual loss gives rise to sorrow; while each of these situations is likely to arouse anger. The unchallenged maintenance of a bond is experienced as a source of security and the renewal of a bond as a source of joy." (p. 40).

The desire to obtain the attachment is always present even after the relationship is severed. When detachment occurs, there are traces of grief and a strong urge to become reattached.

Attachment Theory and Heroin

Bowlby (1969, 1980) describes attachment as physical and psychological. The individual who is beginning his / her recovery phase of treatment often goes through intense anxiety when the bond is beginning to break between the individual and his / her drug of choice. The recovering addict often has strong feelings for the drug of choice and may become distraught at the beginning of the recovery phase of treatment. The individual not able to detach from the drug will follow through with attachment type of behavior to continue the bond of addiction. As a result of the continued desire for attachment the individual will most likely revert to the addiction lifestyle and a relapse may occur. The recovering addict is attempting to discover new coping mechanisms; however, since the emotional bond with the heroin is very intense the individual has difficulty developing coping skills without the drug of choice.

Francis, Keiser and Deaver (2003) completed a study on representations of attachment through drawings of a bird's nest with 70 substance abuse participants in a psychiatric clinic. The research instruments were the Bird's Nest Drawing used to tap emotional issues especially surrounding expectations and The Relationship Questionnaire. There was a difference in the proportion of attachment styles. Non-substance abusers and known to be secure individuals used more color. The themes for the secure individuals were home family, the wonder of nature, the renewal of life, food, or hunger. For substance abusers, a theme of abandonment appeared more frequently. The picture was a nest drawn with no family surrounding the nest. The nest was usually colored in black and white and the sense of security and family ties were not available. The individuals recovering from substance abuse expressed that without the substance they felt abandoned, however, with the substance they felt secure based on their drawings. This study is an illustration of the long-term effects of substances on an individual's life and how attachment plays a major role in addiction and recovering from addiction.

CHAPTER II
REVIEW OF THE LITERATURE

There is limited literature in the area of heroin addiction and grief, however, in the 1980's and the early 1990's there was some research in the area of alcohol recovery and grief and loss issues. As a result, I will be discussing the grief and loss issues related to alcohol that may be relevant to heroin recovery. This literature review will encompass the process of recovery from heroin and alcohol addition, a review of the grieving process, relapse prevention and a combination of grief and loss issues in the recovery stage of addiction. This literature will also discuss the issues surrounding ending a relationship.

Recovering from heroin addiction

An individual attempting to recover from heroin addiction has many emotional challenges to contend with and one such emotion is stress. According to Krueger (1981) stressful life events are the main contributor to an individual relapsing. In his study Krueger studied 270 ex-users and discussed the various events that made them return to the use of heroin. Forty-eight of the sample of 270 returned to heroin at least once during his / her recover period. Krueger studied the relationship between stressful life events and the onset of heroin use for subjects who relapsed within six months using the Zung Depression Scale (1965) and the Social Readjustment Rating Scale (1967). The results showed that individuals who had experienced stressors such as a recent loss or depression had difficulty adjusting to a new lifestyle without the use of heroin. The relapse group had significantly higher scores on the Social Readjustment Rating Scale than those individuals that continued their abstinence. The individuals that scored high on the Social Readjustment Rating Scale had difficulty repositioning in society. According to Krueger, the implications of this study were there might be a relationship between daily life events and relapse in heroin users. Forty-eight participants used heroin as an adaptive attempt to regulate and to control intense and overwhelming anxiety, depression, and to attempt to effectively handle stressful events. The participants stated that when the drug was administered it relieved feelings of depression, shame, hurt and loneliness. The participants stated that heroin was used when needed in stressful times.

Walters (1994) examined the balance between stressors and coping in 120 inmates enrolled in a drug treatment program using the Drug Lifestyle Screening Interview, a 23 item structured interview conceived for the purposes of assessing the four primary behavioral characteristics of the lifestyle of a drug abuser. The four characteristics were irresponsibility, coping imbalance, interpersonal triviality, and rule breaking and bending. The result showed that the stress / coping imbalance occur as a result of lifestyle changes during the recovery stage. Therefore, when individuals are in recovery, they have not fully developed stress mangement without the use of heroin. As a result when stressful life events occur the individual will inadvertently return to heroin as a coping mechanism since the heroin has been a coping mechanism when dealing with problems of everyday living.

Ojesjo (2000) did a follow-up study on 23 individuals involved in the Lundby Project in Sweden. The Lundby Project followed 41 males for 40 years. By the time Ojesjo conducted his study only 23 subjects were still living, 12 of whom had successfully recovered from alcohol addiction and 11 of whom were current problem drinkers. The study reported that negative social circumstances and social pressure to stop drinking were the main causes that the sober individuals discontinued drinking. However, the individuals that had relapsed stated that medical problems, mental problems, family pressure, and work related stressors contributed to their relapse. The participants involved in the study stated that they were able to stay clean because social stabilization, lengthy treatments such as halfway houses, and encouragement from family and friends.

Besides recovering individuals having trouble with stress, they also have trouble with the attempt to change during their recovery. The need to change and the readiness to change is vital for the individual attempting to recover from substance abuse. Blume and Schmaling (1996) completed a study on the readiness to change in recovery with 110 consecutive psychiatric inpatient admissions at an urban hospital using the Cut down, Annoyed, Guilty and Eye Opener (CAGE) given upon admission, along with the Readiness to Change Questionnaire and The Losses of Significant Self-Report Questionnaire. The participants reported many losses and that these losses resulted in them questioning continuing recovery. Blume and Schmaling concluded that a recovering addict having difficulty going through the grieving process may contemplate change. The study concluded that the death of a loved one or any significant loss during the recovery period, may lead to relapse if coping and stress management is not put in place in the early stages of recovery.

Bammer and Weekes (1994) interviewed 18 people during their recovery period to inquire what mechanisms were in place to encourage sobriety. The findings included that people stopped using their drug of choice because of a change environment, falling in love with someone and wanting to be clean to experience the feelings, and wanting to be a positive role model for the children by changing the lifestyle and not exposing the children to drug activity. Some other findings included that some ex-drug users became counselors and enjoyed helping others, and found employment and wanted to keep their job. One participant was very proud that he was working daily and was able to legally register his vehicle in his name and actually pay for the registration. This participant stated he could not have accomplished this unless he was clean. This study gave a good example of how an individual is able to continue sobriety positively.

Gossop, Stewart, Duncan, Browne and Marsden (2002) studied factors that were associated with abstinence in 242 clients from 23 residential programs in the United Kingdom who used heroin before treatment and were followed 12 months after discharge. The participants in this study were given private face-to-face interviews asking questions about problems coping with life events without the use of heroin. Sixty percent of the 242 used heroin after treatment with the first occasion being three days following treatment. The participants that stayed completely abstinent used sound coping strategies such as support groups when experiencing stress or reorganizing their lives to decrease stress and stayed in treatment longer to have total abstinence.

Grief and Loss in Addiction

According to Tiebout (1946) an individual recovering from alcohol must become aware of his / her condition and suffer through the realization and the barriers that were the result of alcohol consumption. The barriers that are inevitable include, but are not limited to, a lack of family support, loss of employment, and loss of the alcohol all of which will interfere in the recovery process. During the suffering of these realizations the recovering alcoholic will grieve these losses, since they are an important piece of their life prior and during addiction.

According to Kaczkowski and Zygmond (1991) an individual recovering from alcohol addiction suffers many losses such as loss of friends, significant others, and loss of the alcohol substance. Kaczkowski and Zygmond studied how individuals recovering from alcohol abuse dealt with the losses. Their results indicate that if recovering addicts do not recognize the losses mentioned above they will experience loss conflict that lessens the chance for a positive recovery. The three factors that were discussed in the results that inhibit passage through the grief process are fear, narcissism, and the failure to distinguish between grief and depression. Kaczkowski and Zygmond concluded that an individual needs to resolve the losses and go through the grieving process by identifying and accepting these losses, expressing the feelings of the loss during inpatient rehabilitation, and develop healthy relationships to be successful in recovery. Finally the researchers state that to deal with an individual in the first stage of recovery, mental health counselors need to respond to clients as they would to other clients who have lost a significant other.

Beechem, Prewitt and Scholar (1996) conducted a group study of 98 substance abusers in an outpatient facility. The study resulted in a grief and loss inventory that examined pre-addiction losses, losses associated with addiction, and losses associated with entering treatment. The results of the grief / loss inventory indicated that some patients were silently dealing with unresolved grief during treatment. The researchers concluded that this grief / loss inventory was an effective guide for therapists to assist clients that are experiencing these losses to develop appropriate coping strategies for a successful recovery. The categories of losses that were discovered from the study: loss of self-respect, loss of a goal or a dream, loss of time, loss of trust in others, loss of financial stability, loss of freedom of choice(s), loss of confidence in others, loss of self-trust, loss of self – confidence and loss of respect from others.

Relationships

As an infant or an adult the detachment of a relationship is very disheartening and can cause grief. According to Helmlinger (1977) ending a relationship after forming an attachment / bond has an emotional impact. The impact can be on an individual's psyche, physical self or both simultaneously.

Helmlinger (1977) examined the results of an adult relationship ending. Through her qualitative research she noticed that ending a relationship went through the Kubler –Ross (1969) grief stages of denial, anger sorrow / despair, depression, bargaining and acceptance. Helmlinger, however took the grieving process one or two steps further. She studied the long – term effects on the person ending the relationship and the healing process when the relationship is slowly dissolving. Helmlinger studied the individual ending the relationship redefining his / her world without the other person and how these emotions are handled. She concluded an individual that has ended a relationship may encounter: loss of self-esteem, loss of identity and living structure, loss of ambition / indecision, and loss of friends and familiar surroundings. Upon ending a relationship an individual may overwhelm him or herself with self –doubt or feelings of inadequacy. According to Helmlinger these emotions can be a salient factor to depression.

Loss of Identity and Living Structure

When a relationship has ended an individual may lose the identity that he / she has been comfortable with for many years. The person may feel that he / she is going through an identity crisis, which soon is followed by an adjustment. The change of a living structure could be going from living with an attached partner, then living alone. The change to now being alone can create fear along with uncertainty about ending the relationship. An individual that has ended the relationship may notice the amount of dependence he or she had on the partner. The individual will learn the need to make decisions interdependent of the partner.

Loss of friends and familiar surroundings

When ending a relationship the acquaintances, familiar surroundings, activities and friends that the person identifies with come to an end. The individual will soon realize that changes will need to be made in his / her life, in particular redefining surroundings and creating a new circle of friends or acquaintances.

Khantzian, Mack and Schatzberg (1974) conducted a qualitative study of six case studies. Each individual interviewed had a diagnosis of heroin addiction and each participant was asked to describe his or her feeling toward the drug. The results of the qualitative study shows that: heroin was loved as much as a significant other, there was a feeling of unity with other heroin users, there was enjoyment in being a accepted as part of a subculture and rituals of paraphernalia of heroin users, heroin was used as a coping strategy, there was an increase of confidence when using the drug, and finally that they were able to adapt to the overwhelming feelings and emotions with the use of heroin.

Summary

The conclusion that the review of literature leads to is, one, is there is a need for research on the effects of grief / loss for substance abusers and two, therapy is important in the early recovery stage from heroin addiction. It is evident that the recovering addict faces obstacles of loss, grief, and needs to develop appropriate coping skills for a productive recovery.

There needs to be more research in the area of substance abuse and the relationship that the user has created between him / herself and the drug. The literature describes the emotional pain when two humans separate in a relationship; there has been limited research to illustrate the significance of the relationship between the addict and his / her drug of choice. This study will examine how the relationship is formed and the emotional changes that occur when the relationship between the user and the drug is threatened or ends. This study will examine strategies a therapist may use to effectively counsel addicts with unresolved grief and loss issues related to heroin addiction.

CHAPTER III
METHODS AND PROCEDURES

This third chapter consists of methods and procedures for this study. A description of the participants and the demographic information will be given along with a description of the site where the study was conducted. This chapter also provides detailed information regarding the instrument used prior to the interviews, the general research questions, the interview questions and the analysis of the data using grounded theory.

Participants

The criteria of the participation in this study were that all participants needed to be in the detoxification phase of treatment and be willing to complete detoxification; along with the ability to speak English for the audio-taped interview as well as for completing the Ways of Coping Questionnaire since an interpreter is not provided in this study. The detoxification phase of treatment is when a patient is admitted to a facility and is given methadone to safely detoxify from the heroin (opiate) misuse.

The admission's nurse and the patient's case manager recruited participants for the study. Upon admission, the patients were informed of the study by the admission's nurse and were given an opportunity to volunteer for the study. The patient informed the admission's nurse of their interest, and the patient's name was given to the assistant director. The assistant director gave the names to me and I explained the study to the patients.

Fourteen individuals volunteered for the study; however two individuals dropped out so 12 participants were included. The demographic breakdown of the 12 participants is: eight males and four females; 2 married, 8 single, 1 widowed, 1 divorced. The method of use for the heroin: 9 Intravenous use, 1 nasal, 1 skin popping and 1 oral. The ethnicity / race of the participants: 1 African American, 2 Hispanic, and 9 White.

All 12 participants had a heroin (opiate) dependence diagnosis made upon admission to the inpatient facility. The diagnosis of "opiate dependent" was determined by the admission's nurse according to the results of a urinalysis taken by the patient. The participants were also given a health and physical assessment by the Family Nurse Practitioner (FNP) to determine the dependence as well as other medical problems. All persons entering the hospital had blood drawn to determine any medical issues that would need immediate attention. Two participants that were part of this study were identified as having hepatitis C. The participants were referred to outside medical appointments for follow-up of the hepatitis C diagnosis, which did not affect their participation in the study.

Site

This study took place at BryLin Hospitals Addiction Medicine Inpatient Unit, a leader in the area of psychiatric, addiction medicine and behavior health services in the Buffalo area since 1955. Over the years, this facility specialized in opiate detoxification using methadone and auricular acupuncture. The hospital was chosen for the study because there was a large population of individuals attending the hospital for opiate detoxification and rehabilitation. The population of opiate dependent clients at BryLin Hospitals was approximately 25% of the 62-bed inpatient facility. Unfortunately at the time of the study, the hospital staff and the patients were informed that the Alden site would be closing. At the time that BryLin Hospitals was chosen for the study, I was not aware that the unit would be closing.

Data Sources

The research questions were proposed to investigate the emotional feelings that the recovering heroin – addict experiences in an inpatient facility during early recovery and his / her coping mechanisms. The general research questions for this qualitative study are: 1. What are the losses experienced by the addict when first entering treatment? 2. How do the addicts cope with these losses as well as losses in the past?

There were two data sources for this study, the Ways of Coping Questionnaire and the interview questions.

Each participant was required to complete the Ways of Coping Questionnaire by Folkman and Lazarus (1988) prior to the interview. The purpose of this questionnaire was to stimulate the participants' thinking processes prior to the face - to - face interview. The questionnaire specifically examines stressful situations that require the client to react and to utilize coping mechanisms. This questionnaire consisted of 63 statements on a four point Likert-type scale. The four choices that the participants had for each of the 63 statements were: "not at all," "used somewhat," "used quite a bit," "used a great deal." There were eight coping scales with internal consistency reliabilities ranging from .61 to .79. Each of the eight coping scales was used. Each coping scale consisted of its own definition to describe the way a person copes with a situation according to Folkman and Lazarus (1988). The eight coping scales and their definitions are: 1) confrontive coping describes the individual taking the opportunity to make an effort to change a situation with hostility as well as risk – taking behaviors; 2) distancing involves the effort to detach from a situation; 3) self-controlling is the behavior evident that an individual takes control of his / her feelings by monitoring actions; 4) seeking social support describes the individual seeking the appropriate level of support which includes, but not limited to emotional support; 5) accepting responsibility is the opportunity that an individual will take to understand his or her role in the situation; 6) escape – avoidance is also described as detachment as well as the behavioral efforts that are used to ignore a situation or problem; 7) planful problem solving involves an individual taking the opportunity to focus on the problems while creating a solution and analyzing the problem; and 8) positive appraisal assesses whether the individual is able to focus on personal growth as well as spirituality.

The second source of data was one face – to – face interview with each participant regarding his / her losses and coping mechanisms (see Appendix B). These questions were asked in four phases. Phase one consists of losses and coping skills prior to addiction; phase two focuses on the addiction and losses along with coping mechanisms; phase three focuses on past sobriety and losses suffered during this time period and the manner in which the participant copes; and phase four focuses on the participant's recent relapse and allowing the participant to project into their future recovery. After the four phases of the interview was complete all participants were debriefed focusing on any distress that may have been caused by the interview. There were no incidents of homicidal or suicidal ideations after the interview and all participants were aware of the resources at the hospital such as counseling and the nursing staff. All participants who were interviewed appeared to be grateful to discuss their drug usage and the effect on their life.

Data Collection

The interview was preceded by the participant's completion of the *Ways of Coping Questionnaire* by Folkman and Lazarus (1988). This measure was used to stimulate the interview process. The participants were given one hour to complete the questionnaire; most of the participants were finished with the questionnaire within a half-hour to forty-five minutes. During the time the eleven participants were completing the measure, I left the room and allowed the participant to complete the questionnaire without any interference. However, I did stay near by to answer any questions or to ethically assist the 11 participants as needed. I stayed in the room and read all questions to one participant because she was blind in one eye.

The entire process that included the completion of the *Ways of Coping Questionnaire* and the face – to – face interview took one and a half hours to two hours for each of the 12 participants.

Analysis of Data

Grounded theory is a type of qualitative data analysis that explores the process of how people solve a problem. Grounded theory formulated by Glaser and Strauss (Glaser, 1978; Strauss & Corbin, 1998), is about conceiving and intuiting ideas by formulating concepts in a logical, systematic, and explanatory scheme from the data collected. The theory is also known as the comparative method because the researcher is constantly analyzing patterns of relationships within the data. Grounded theory's purpose is to closely look at the basic social process of behavior utilized by the participants as a way to resolve a basic social psychological problem that is related to the research question (Glaser, 1978; Strauss & Corbin, 1998).

The principal investigator is able to identify relationships within the data by performing a series of analysis. The first level of analysis is open coding: breaking down, examining, comparing, conceptualizing and categorizing data. This type of analysis is done by extracting sentences or entire paragraphs from interview transcripts. The research question(s) are taken in consideration when beginning to code the data. The result of the open coding is the development of categories derived from the data.

The next step after the open coding is axial coding: linking the categories and developing properties and dimensions of the categories. The dimensions actually identify a variety of conditions, actions and consequences associated with a phenomenon being studied. Axial coding is also relating a category to other categories through statements from the participants describing how the two are related. When looking for links between categories, the theoretical coding "families" described by Glaser (1978) helps the researcher determine connections between categories and whether those connections represent a process, cause and effect, or strategy.

Once the researcher has developed categories and the links between them, a central theme or a core category is identified. This general theme must appear frequently in the data and must also be related to previous categories. This core category / theme must be clear and an indication for a further explanation of the phenomenon.

While the principal investigator is coding the data, developing categories and linking categories, he / she may have questions regarding the data. The researcher will usually write questions or thoughts about the data on a 5x7 card and link the questions to quotations or certain sections of the data. This procedure is "memoing" (Strauss & Corbin, 1998). Memos can also be the researcher's interpretations of the data.

The analysis phase began with my transcribing the audiotapes in Microsoft Word 2003. I then listened to the tapes while reading the transcription to eliminate any errors. Next I exported the 12 interviews from Microsoft Office 2003 into the Atlas.ti software. I then analyzed each interview line by line using the open coding method. I extracted excerpts of data highlighting and giving a code and I also did a memo for the code and the excerpts. Each code was then stored in the coding manager of the software and each memo was stored in the memo manager organized by the code and the excerpt was stored in the quotations manager also organized by the code.

I then began axial coding with the use of the software to develop categories. The development of the categories was done in the network manager of the software by examining the codes produced from the open coding technique and combining like codes. The following categories were developed: 1) Grief and Loss from the heroin, 2) Detaching from the heroin, 3) The attachment to the heroin, 4) The culture of the heroin addiction, 5) The choice to cope by using heroin and 6) Treatment. After these categories were developed, the properties of each category were placed with precision in the network manager. Next the categories with the properties were examined in the family network manager identifying cause and effect relationships, process relationships as well as how the properties are associated with each other in relationship to the category.

The category of attachment to heroin and the category of the culture of heroin were combined to one category the heroin relationship and there were two sub-themes. 1) The development of the relationship with heroin: heroin, heroin culture, heroin lifestyle, and primary relationships (See Figure 1). 2) The components of the heroin relationship: love affair (heroin is controlling), heroin lifestyle, heroin culture, and needle obsession (See Figure 2). Through the interviews I observed the participants having a strong bond and attachment to heroin while in addiction, illustrating the depth of their relationship with heroin.

The categories of grief and loss from heroin and the detachment from heroin were combined to create the category of losses. The sub-themes are: loss of lifestyle, loss of culture, loss of acquaintances, loss of comfort, loss of the drug itself (heroin), loss of enjoyment, loss of needle, and loss of the ritual. The category and the sub-themes are explained in detail with evidence in Chapter 4.

The category, choice to cope by using heroin had the following sub-themes attached: grief (death, trauma), lack of coping skills, and heroin as a means of coping; each of which is explained with evidence in Chapter 4.

The category of treatment was identified, as treatment is not addressing the problem. The sub-themes were: self-help groups, not doing well after treatment, relapsing because of the needle obsession, and relapsing because the feelings about heroin are not discussed. Although, this section has limited data the treatment category and its sub-themes are important to acknowledge. Therefore in Chapter 4 I give evidence that participants would like to continue recovery outside of treatment but do not have the appropriate coping mechanisms.

The main theme for the categories of losses, lack of coping skills and treatment not addressing the problem is: **Ending the relationship with heroin**; and the theory is: **Individuals that are attempting recovery grieve the loss of heroin and its components. If these losses are not addressed, unresolved grief and disenfranchised grief results increasing the likelihood of a relapse.**

CHAPTER IV
RESULTS

This results section incorporates the Ways of Coping Questionnaire (Section 1) results and the ranking of the eight coping scales. There is a slight difference with the ranking of the coping scales done by the original authors and the ranking of the participants in this study. I explain the differences and the interpretation follows. Section 2 discusses in detail the categories and the sub-themes that were outlined in chapter 3. This second section also illustrates the building and the development of the core theme / category and the theory of this study.

Section 1
Ways of Coping Questionnaire Results

The *Ways of Coping Questionnaire* was given to the twelve participants to stimulate the participant's thoughts during the interview. Eleven of the participants answered the questions independently; however, the twelfth participant was blind in one eye and had difficulty reading the sixty-five questions; as a result, the principal investigator read the questions as well as the response choices. The principal investigator used SPSS to input the responses to the sixty-five questions from the eight scales to complete the descriptive statistics. (See Table 1)

Ranking of scales

Combining the two responses, "used quite a bit," and "used a great deal" to generate the extent each coping style was used frequently by the participants; the scales were then ranked in order of use. The ranking of the scales from most used coping mechanism to the least used coping mechanism is: 1. accepting responsibility, 2. confrontive coping, 3. self-controlling, 4. escape-avoidance, 5. seeking social support, 6. distancing, 7. planful problem solving and 8. positive reappraisal.

Table 1 (Ranking the *Ways of Coping Scale*)

Subscale	***Not al all***	***Used Somewhat***	***Used quite a bit***	***Used a great deal***	***Total Scal***
Accepting Responsibility	0%	8%	50%	42%	92%
Confrontive Coping	0%	17%	58%	25%	83%
Self - Controlling	0%	17%	75%	8%	83%
Escape - Avoidance	0%	25%	33%	42%	75%
Seeking Social Support	0%	33%	42%	25%	67%

	8%	25%	41%	25%	66%
Planful Problem Solving	8%	42%	42%	8%	50%
	0%	50%	33%	17%	50%

The *Ways of Coping Questionnaire* provided an opportunity for the participant to identify his / her coping skills. As noted in Table 1, there were four responses for each question from which the participants chose one on each of the sixty-five questions: "not at all used," "used somewhat," "used quite a bit," and "used a great deal." Each scale: confrontive coping, distancing, self-controlling, seeking social support, accepting responsibility, escape – avoidance, planful problem solving and positive reappraisal, will be discussed individually along with some of the individual questions to which most participants responded with "quite a bit," or "a great deal." Along with the highlighting of selected questions, the scales will be ranked on the extent to which the ways of coping they represent were used by the participants.

Accept Responsibility

The accept responsibility scale was ranked as the first most used coping mechanism with 92% of the participants indicating that they accepted responsibility for their addiction. There were four questions in this scale and questions 25, 29 and 51 were answered by 10 of the participants as "used quite a bit," or "used a great deal." Statements that represent this category include: "I apologized or did something to make up," "Realized I brought the problem on myself," "I made a promise to myself that things would be different next time."

Confrontive Coping

The confrontive coping scale ranked as the second most used way of coping. Eighty-three percent of the subjects used confrontive coping "quite a bit" or "a great deal." Participants in this study clearly attempted to cope with addiction by confronting it. There were six questions in this scale and 10 of the participants answered statement 34: "Took a big chance or did something very risky."

Self – Controlling

The self – controlling scale ranked as the third most used coping mechanism with 83% of participants indicating they tried to cope by keeping a tight rein on their feelings. There were seven questions in this scale and two statements were ranked highly by almost all of the participants. Statement 43 was answered by 11 of the participants: "Kept others from knowing how bad things were;" question 62 was answered by 10 of the participants: "I went over in my mind what I would say or do."

Escape – Avoidance

The escape – avoidance scale was ranked as the fourth most used way of coping with 75% of the participants in this study indicating that they used drugs to escape or avoid problems. There were eight questions in this scale and 11 of the participants answered "used quite a bit," or "used a great deal" to statement 33: "Tried to make myself feel better by eating, drinking, smoking, using drugs or medication, etc;" and statement 58: "Wished that the situation would go away or somehow be over with."

Seeking Social Support

The seeking social support scale ranked as the fifth most used coping mechanism with 67% of the participants indicating that they used sought out social support during their addiction. There were six statements in this scale and question 42 was answered by nine of the participants as used "quite a bit" or "used a great deal": "I asked a relative or friend I respected for advice."

Distancing

The distancing scale ranked as the sixth most used way of coping with 66% of the participants saying they tried to distance themselves from their situation in order to cope with the problem. There were six statements in this scale, however, statement 12 and statement 13 were answered by eight of the participants as "used quite a bit," or "used a great deal." "Went along with fate; sometimes I just have bad luck." "Went on as if nothing had happened."

Planful Problem Solving

The planful problem solving scale was ranked as the seventh most used way of coping with 50% of the participants in this study indicating that they lacked problem - solving skills. There were six statements in this scale and eight participants answered "used quite a bit," or "used a great deal" for statement 39: "Changed something so things would turn out all right;" and statement 52: "Came up with a couple of different solutions to the problem."

Positive Reappraisal

The positive reappraisal scale ranked as the least used way of coping with 50% of the participants in the study indicating that positive reappraisal was not used often as a coping mechanism. There were seven statements in this scale and three statements were answered "used quite a bit," or "used a great deal:" statement 36 was answered by nine participants, "Found new faith;" statement 38 was answered by nine participants, "Rediscovered what was important in life." Statement 60 was answered by ten participants, "I prayed."

This questionnaire appeared to allow the participants to re-examine their coping skills or lack of coping skills. Participant four stated, "Wow I see I lack coping skills." Participant 11 stated, "I thought about how I have handled losing my girlfriend and other losses by always using heroin, I need more coping skills." Participant three stated, "This made me think about how I have not coped with my father's death and how I keep using to numb my feelings."

These results suggest that the participants in this study accept responsibility, however lack the coping skills to appropriately manage stress. The participants in this study coped with stress by using heroin and this was apparent in the results of the questionnaire, and the interview results.

Section 2
Interview Results

The participants in this study were all involved with the detoxification stage of treatment and all of the participants had been involved in treatment more than once during their journey of addiction. The analysis of the interviews resulted in the common theme that there is a relationship between the addict and the drug that bonds him / her with the many facets of heroin addiction. The participants in this study expressed that heroin was their primary focus while in active addiction. The participants in this study discussed the way in which their relationship with the heroin developed and progressed prior to attending a detoxification facility.

During the addiction, the addict may have suffered losses by heroin addiction, such as family, employment, and / or material items; these losses, however, were not of primary importance while in active addiction, the heroin, the culture, and the lifestyle had taken precedence (See Figure 1).

Figure 1 (Development of the heroin relationship)

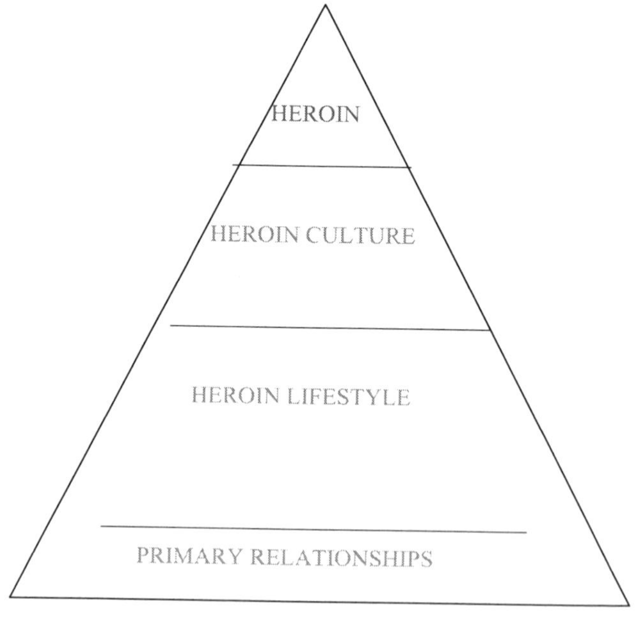

As addicts become more involved with heroin they are forming bonds that will eliminate the past primary relationships such as a spouse, children, or close friends. The addict soon becomes enmeshed in the heroin culture and the daily routine becomes seeking the drug and using to avoid withdrawal symptoms as explained in Chapter 1.

According to the data heroin takes precedence and becomes the addict's main focus. During addiction the addict becomes more involved with the heroin culture resulting in a progressive relationship with the heroin that involves four components. This relationship has enmeshed characteristics of love affair with heroin, the lifestyle, the culture, and the needle obsession / ritual. These four parts of the relationship (see Figure 2) are vital to the heroin addict and once the addict enters treatment all of these components are taken away creating a void in the addict's life and a significant loss.

Figure 2 (Components of the heroin relationship)

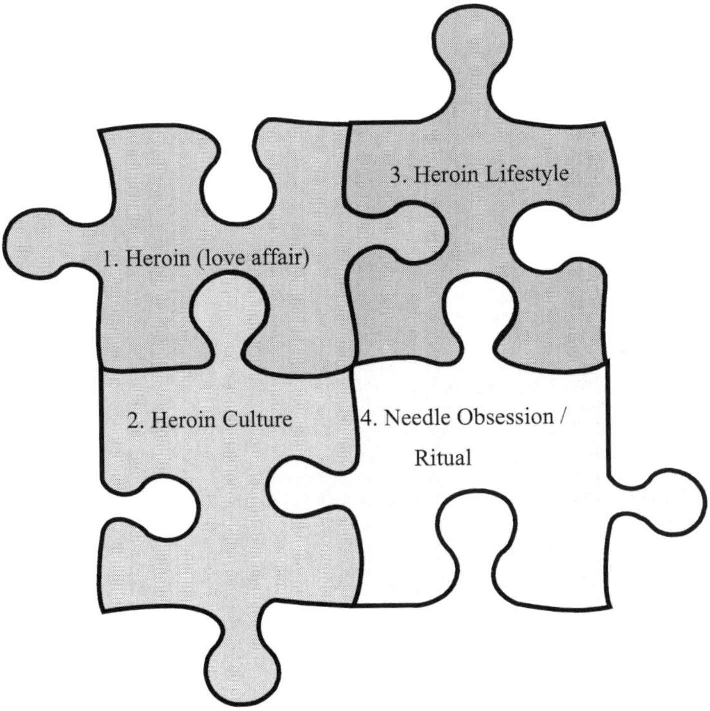

3. Heroin Lifestyle

1. Heroin (love affair)

2. Heroin Culture

4. Needle Obsession / Ritual

The development of the heroin relationship is very intense. Upon entering treatment the addict suffers not just the loss of the drug, but all the components that the addict has been attached to for many months or years. This section describes the participants feelings toward the loss of this relationship. The theme that emerged from the data was that **the relationship with heroin is ending**. The theory is: **Individuals that are attempting recovery, grieve the loss of heroin and its components. If these losses are not addressed, unresolved and disenfranchised grief results increasing the likelihood of relapse.**

The three categories from the analysis of the data were: losses, coping, and treatment is not addressing the problem of ending the relationship with heroin.

Losses

As mentioned earlier in Chapter 2, an individual who has lost a relationship goes through a period of grief when reminiscing about the parts of the relationship that had some significance. The individual may also have problems with his / her identity because it was wrapped up in the relationship. Heroin addicts have the same dilemma, they have an identity of being a "junkie" as well as being around a certain crowd that provides a sense of belonging and comfort while in active addiction. The addict who makes the choice to enter treatment for detoxification is detaching himself / herself from the heroin culture and lifestyle and for the participants in this study it was a painful decision to separate from the heroin.

The participants were questioned if they felt a loss for the drug. The majority of the participants agreed that losing the heroin was significant since they had become attached to the heroin. The heroin resembled a best friend for some and signified a lover for others. Ultimately the heroin has become a way of life for the addict and to begin separation while in treatment can be traumatic for an individual now entering treatment. Besides the loss of heroin the individual admits that there is a loss of the other three components: lifestyle, culture, and needle / ritual. There is also a loss of comfort and enjoyment. These losses result in grief and for the recovering addict that is going through the stages of grief there is room for hating the heroin. The participants in this study expressed that they did not hate the drug itself, but the consequences and the negative results from the drug usage. The data illustrated that for the most part these participants grieved in silence resulting in unresolved grief and when the participant does not discuss this grief or are not allowed to grieve the drug and its components the result is disenfranchised grief.

Loss of heroin

The participants in this study expressed that losing heroin was a difficult task and felt like losing a best friend or a lover. The participants discussed the drug with such emotion that it was obvious that the attachment to the heroin was still present. Heroin has become such an important part of the addict's life that nothing is done without the accompaniment of heroin: "I don't know what to do or what am I going to do, I need to find what I love, it has been such a way of life for me." (Participant 10) "It's going to be miserable; it's all I'm going to think about, I'm going to obsess over it [heroin]." (Participant 8) Heroin has become such an important part of the participant's life that after treatment the attempt to find something that will be just as satisfying seems to be unreachable for him during this time in treatment.

The attachment to heroin for the participants was expressed as a love affair:

> It was like a love affair plan and simple. The only other thing that I could compare it to was the love that I had for my mom and my girlfriend. I mean it was even more so than that, I mean I could go a couple of days without seeing my mother or girlfriend but I wouldn't go a couple of days without seeing the heroin guy to get my dope. It controlled me and literally it ran the show in my life. No if ands or buts about it. (Participant 11)

This participant expressed his love for the heroin similar to the love for a significant other or a parent except that there was a desire to see the heroin daily. He expressed that this love was very controlling. Now that the participant is in treatment, he is able to understand the controlling; but he is still expressing a love for the drug.

The participants were asked "*Do you feel a loss now that heroin is not in your life*?" This question was important since the recovering addict depended on the drug for many of life's situations, it is important to understand how the recovering addict plans to live his / her life. Participant 3 was very emotional about the loss since the heroin has become such a significant part of this participant's life.

> Ah man I don't know, I almost bounced last night because I was just like why am I here. And even as I sit here and I am talking about this and the experiences, I probably will use again. It really breaks my heart (tears). I know I am going to use again. (Participant 3)

This addict sadly expressed that the loss of heroin was too great and she considered leaving the treatment facility to use heroin. She was expressing that the loss is so great that the determination that heroin will be used again was inevitable. The participant has lived her life surrounded with heroin that she appeared to feel empty and lost without the drug in her life. This emptiness encouraged the urge to use the drug and to become reacquainted with the comfort. She admits in this above quote that she was ready to leave treatment to satisfy the urge to use. The participant, however, continued treatment, but appeared to be torn between recovery and relapsing.

While a participant is in treatment he / she begins to detoxify from the opiates and it is during this phase of treatment when the participants stated that they realized the loss of heroin or other significant relationships. "I feel the loss of my girlfriend, or ex-girlfriend I lost because of my use. When I was using I didn't give a s___ but now I feel the losses and that [heroin] included." (Participant 8) He is realizing that two significant relationships are now diminished. The heroin is now gone because of a decision and the significant other is gone because of the heroin use. Now that sobriety is present for this participant he has come to recognize that there is a loss of the drug as well as of his significant other.

The participants in this study often stated that "letting go" of the heroin or the opiate pills is difficult, but that one does not know this until he / she has entered treatment:

> Just the same as a loss of a friend or a person – but it's almost even harder to let go. Because of that feeling that you love so much you know maybe I loved that more – I haven't really dealt with something that I love so much die yet. You know my father and my brother. Everyone that I love to death hasn't passed away fortunately. So I have the pills, I like them, I love them you could say what else can I say. It's just like any other grieving process, yea I'm gonna miss it, but the whole difference is I'm not grieving death because it is still there and you know you can get it. With death you know that it is gone so you have to deal with that and drugs you have to fight it because you know that they are there. It's a hard thing and I think that is the difference between grieving a loved-one and grieving the pill even though I loved the pills. But they are still there. (Participant 7)

This participant is grieving the loss of the opiate pills and went as far to say that heroin was loved and cherished more than other relationships. He grieves the opiate and has the understanding that the opiate can be used again; that is an individual can relapse. He is struggling with the love for the opiate and the desire to be clean and has expressed that it is very difficult to separate from the opiate.

Participant 10 expresses the loss of heroin was similar to losing a best friend:

> It feels like you lose a best friend it totally does. I don't really have a long time being clean, but I am missing the drug a lot. I was thinking of the times that I would be getting high with this person and I was thing of old times and good times. These felt good to me I miss that day. I want at the bottom of my heart I want to get clean, but if you put it right in front of me right now, I wouldn't say no. It's really hard.

This addict relates missing the drug to missing something that she enjoyed and that felt "good" to her. She misses the drug a lot considering that she was in treatment. She was very certain that if the heroin were offered, she would use it. This shows that there is a conflict between the desire to get clean and the continued desire to use the drug. She expressed that the desire to use the drug would override the desire to be clean and expressed the difficulty of letting go of the drug and choosing sobriety.

Loss of comfort

The participants in this study expressed a feeling of comfort connected to using heroin. They described their use of heroin as generating a warm feeling and a feeling of security. The addict that has come into treatment will lose the reliability and the security that heroin provided, the addict will need to discover another activity that provides comfort without the physical and psychological consequences:

> I grieve the comfort, and the reliability that it is always there. It always made me feel better even if I had a sore throat you know what I mean. I'm just a sucker toward pain. I would say I would do a bag, you know it is so silly, but that is just the way it is. (Participant 3)

This participant has stated that heroin provided a feeling of comfort. This comfort feeling is the part of losing heroin that the addicts seem to grieve the most. Heroin has an effect of putting the addict at ease when there are difficult circumstances. The addict that has experienced this feeling of comfort will expect this feeling each time that he / she uses the drug. However, now that the addict has made a decision to discontinue using the drug, other measures of comfort need to be created. The addict is losing something he / she has come to depend on.

This sense of comfort that the heroin provides for the addict also provides a sense of confidence, for some of the participants in the study doing daily activities was impossible unless heroin was administered:

> I like heroin it is as simple as that. You can take away anything from me, but I will use that little bit in the morning. I feel like I can do the dishes. I can sew. Without it I can't come out. (Participant 12)

The participants in this study made it very clear that, when heroin was used they did not have any concerns. For example, participant 7 noted, "It made me not worry and not care it made me feel good and speed me up kind of." The addict that has come into treatment loses the mechanism that has been used each time there is a worry or a concern. The addict has fallen back on the drug for many months or many years and while the individual is attempting treatment it takes all the recovering addict can muster not return to the heroin.

Heroin was used as a comforter, as one would find in a best friend: "Well, it was like my best friend that comforted me." (Participant 5) The addict needs to develop support systems other than the heroin. This adaptation takes a while since the individual had been surviving this way for many months or years:

> As for the heroin it is hard to explain, let's see, when you've been sober for like a year and you do that first shot and you feel that it is like being in the arms of an angel. Angel will wrap its wings around you. Any pain, I mean your wrist might hurt, I've broken a lot of bones over the years it's just everything goes away. To be honest with you, if I could have a lifetime supply on the radio or a game show I wouldn't quit. If it wasn't a financial difficulty I wouldn't care what happened. I mean if I could grow my own poppies and have enough to get through the harvest, I would never quit. (Participant 11)

This addict expressed that the comfort felt by the heroin resembles the arms of an angel. This feeling of comfort offers a sense of security that the participant desires to continue. The heroin addicts that come into treatment may have a desire to be clean, but desire that competes with the need to feel comfort. According to this participant, if this feeling of comfort could continue without consequences and there was enough supply his use would continue. For most addicts that come into treatment, there is a strong desire to continue to use because of the benefits that the addict is receiving; however, the consequences are too great, the addict will then force himself / herself to attend treatment and attempt to overcome the desire to continue using. The addict has two sides to his / her life when entering treatment. There is the side that would like to change because the result of using has created a disaster, yet on the other side, the addict wants to continue the use because the heroin provides a safety net. The addict in treatment will struggle with creating a new safety net with less turmoil.

The participants in this study that were serious about ending the relationship with heroin appeared to struggle with the comfort that was felt during the active addiction. The participants that mentioned the comfort seemed to be uncomfortable with beginning recovery. The participants appeared lost and did not know how to replace this feeling that heroin provided.

Loss of enjoyment

The participants in this study as a whole were very attached to the aroused feeling that they received from heroin. The participants described the feeling when using the heroin with such raw emotion that the attachment was apparent. "Yea, it is a feeling. The heroin, I don't like the way it looks or tastes. I'm just hooked on a feeling. It's like I'm hooked on feeling – everything could be wrong and I use and feel all right." (Participant 11) He is stating that the feeling that the heroin provides is one reason that he continues to use the drug. The feeling that all is well with the addict's life even if all is not well, using the heroin gives the feeling that there are no concerns; this is the feeling that the heroin addict enjoys.

The participants in this study often stated the euphoria was the part of using that would be missed when entering treatment: "That feeling is a big part, the euphoria, not worrying about the problems or issues and all of that." (Participant 7) The euphoric feeling is the result of an individual using the drug and this feeling happens each time an individual uses the drug:

> The feeling of, it's like feeling good, it's a feeling like you're in heaven, feeling like everything around you is a different world. It's a world of relaxation. Now the feeling is not there no more – now you have to chase the monkey. (Participant 4)

This participant is describing the feeling that heroin addicts have prior to treatment and how much they have to struggle with the feeling that they have found, enjoyment. The participants express that even in recovery the desire for that feeling is still within the recovering addict, and the thoughts that society has are not favorable. As a result, the addict struggles silently within:

> Heroin I used, I don't know I used it to block pain and it gave me this significant feeling, how do you say it took me under. Heroin took me under and you know once you're into the active use of heroin it seems like all good side is gone. You go through the withdrawals and it is not fun and ah for me I had to have some type of higher power to get me through, I had a little faith I was at the point where I had lost a lot of hope but I always had a little faith, always no matter how bad I felt I always felt like something good was going to happen. (Participant 9)

Despite the fact that the heroin gave a good feeling this participant is struggling with the attempt to recover from heroin. This participant was able to understand that the continued use of heroin had consequences that were so great that the participant had hope that the recovery would be successful. The feeling that the participants expressed does not seem to disappear once the addict enters treatment or even completes treatment. The feeling of using is imbedded in the psyche of the recovering addict, which creates a strain when in treatment. The recovering addict is attempting to recover, but the thought of the euphoric feeling, the feeling of relaxation is constantly racing through the recovering addict's mind.

The recovering addict that is attempting recovery struggles with the ability to use heroin once again. The recovering addict presently weighs the consequences to convince himself / herself to not use the drug. For the participants in this study this was a reality since there has been past failed attempts at recovery.

"I know the consequences of it, and once you go back to it – I know that there's hospitals, death and prison, loss of family, and that is very painful. But I like it." (Participant 4) "It's a feeling you can't describe, it just takes everything away, all your pain all your feeling and you don't care about anything." (Participant 5) Despite the consequence and the reality of losses, the recovering addict admits that liking the heroin is still a priority. The recovering addict has expressed that all of the losses and the consequences are painful; however, the heroin is still a prodigious part of the life and mind of the recovering addict.

The recovering addict continues his / her struggle to not use heroin but often finds pleasure in reminiscing about past use. The past is usually remembered as an enjoyable feeling. The participants in this study often reminisced on the feeling, which they described as positive. The participants seldom reminisced on the negative, meaning the physical withdrawal symptoms: "Yes, I miss being high sometimes; I miss that warm fuzzy feeling sometime like an angel..." (Participant 11) This participant is expressing that while in the recovery stage, the participant is missing the loss of the heroin and the loss of the feeling. The participant describes the feeling as warm feeling; this can be compared to the sense of comfort and security that the addict feels during addiction. Despite the desire to be clean, now there is a void and the good feeling and the sense of security is not present because heroin is absent from the recovering addict's life.

There were some participants in the study that enjoyed the feeling of heroin, but began to hate the drug while in treatment. Hating the drug, however, is not connected to the good feelings the drug inspires, but rather it is connected to the consequences of continued use. The consequences of continued use were returning to a detoxification facility, prison, or institutions. The participant would take responsibility, but hated the drug for the results. "I don't miss that drug, I hate it, but I keep going back to it." (Participant 4)

This participant was struggling with the fact that he "hates" heroin, but continues to use the drug. This participant did not disclose his reasons, but one can speculate that the drug was used as a coping mechanism.

The grieving process that the recovering addict goes through has hate as well as anger toward the drug. Participant 6 shared that he was angry at the drug and most of all angry at his decision to return to heroin: "I feel angry at it because I got back on it I can't believe I did it again, I relapsed. I feel like a big loser, I feel like I messed up." (Participant 6) The participant showed emotions at the drug as if it were a human being. The participant is also angry because a relapse occurred from his last attempt at recovery. When the recovering addict continues attempts at sobriety, but fails the result may be hating the heroin as well as hating the consequences.

Loss of culture

The culture of heroin users is related to the socialization related to the addiction. The socialization entails the people that the addict associates with while in active addiction. For some of the recovering heroin addicts this culture is the only secular of people that were accepting and "loving." When the recovering addict detaches from the culture it is a loss that is grieved since the addict has used the majority of his / her time building these relationships that surrounded the heroin.

The participants of this study openly discussed with me the parts of the heroin culture that make heroin addiction different than other addictions. They expressed that the heroin culture includes drug acquaintances, rituals, and needle obsession. The participants in this study expressed that these components of the culture were different than other drugs because being involved in the culture was comforting and formed a bond with other heroin addicts. Participant 5 notes that, "I think heroin addicts feel this bond with each other more than other people who use different substances. It's a weird type of click with these people." This participant is stating that the heroin addicts identify with each other and form a clique that is different from other substances. The ability to identify with another heroin addict regarding the emotions that present themselves during the addiction is comforting and allows the addict to bond. This gives credence to the addiction and the socialization. When the addict makes a decision to attend treatment the she / he is walking away from the heroin culture and all its components. This detachment may not be easy for some addicts, because addiction has been the only place where he / she felt accepted. The support that other addicts give in the heroin culture at times may be the only support that the addict had ever felt. Addicts that make a choice to detach from the drug are also detaching from the heroin culture, thus forcing themselves the need to create a new way of socializing and to develop acceptance with sober individuals through one's own abilities rather than by using a drug.

Loss of Lifestyle / drug acquaintances (drug family)

The lifestyle of heroin users is related to the manner used to obtain and maintain their addiction. The lifestyle includes the neighborhood that the addict might frequent to purchase their drug. The lifestyle also includes the activity used to obtain the heroin, which equates to chaos. The participants in this study alluded to not only being addicted to heroin, but also being addicted to the chaos of the addiction. The participants in the study that used alone, because of work obligations or fear that they would be recognized purchasing drugs, did not miss the lifestyle, they only missed the benefits of the drug. However, the participants that did create a lifestyle around purchasing the drug and being involved in the environment of addiction discussed openly their emotions toward the lifestyle and the acquaintances involved.

> Yes, absolutely yes. People must think that I am crazy. They have said what do you miss about going on the west side. That is what I did every morning for years and years and years. I miss coppin' Spanish to the Puerto Ricans, I learned how to say my drug and I learned to say how much I wanted. Even the cat calls you know what I mean, as much as you don't want to hear it at least you feel good as a woman. I mean that is what I did since the age of 17 years old everyday, all day long. I would scam go cop then go steal, then go cop you know what I mean, I mean what else is there to do. (Participant 3)

This participant is expressing that missing the lifestyle entails missing the people that are associated with the heroin. She also missed the environment where the drugs were purchased. The heroin addicts that are attempting recovery often reminisce on the environment where they used or purchased the drug. The idea of copping or buying the drug in a certain part of a neighborhood was exciting for this participant. She states that the cat calls while in the lifestyle of addiction made her feel good as a woman. While in addiction, especially heroin, one can have low self-esteem, however, this participant depended on a false sense of esteem while in the lifestyle of addiction. This participant expressed that she had been involved with this lifestyle since her teen years and it appears that she is lost without this lifestyle and has not explored other options.

As mentioned earlier the culture is embracing for some people in addiction. The lifestyle and those involved are embracing also. There are some recovering addicts that also embrace their supplier of the drug and appear excited reminiscing about this person and his / her role in the addict's life while in active addiction. Participant 8 explained:

> I miss the part of going to cop and going to T's parking lot and getting high on the west side. I miss the dealer, I miss their face opening the door – meaning I got what I want now, I miss that. They're the people that make my day.

The addict that is missing the lifestyle because it was such a priority in the daily activity is actually grieving the lifestyle in particular this participant has expressed he that misses his dealer. The participant is also missing the surrounding areas that he administered the drug.

There are some parts of the lifestyle that may appear in treatment, such as music. The recovering addict may also begin to reminisce his / her addiction because of the music. Music is part of the heroin addict's life while using because there may be a certain type of music or a song that reminds him / her of the use of heroin. Participant 8 gives an account of music and how it is interfering in his recovery:

> Yea, I missed the city music with the bumps kickin' in. I can't listen to music anymore unless I am using or else I want to use – music is my disease I think. Rap music – so it's the music that makes me want to use – I think music is what brings me to usin'. (Participant 8)

This participant is tempted to use heroin by the sound of music and in particular rap music. He has admitted that listening to rap music is a trigger to use heroin since use always occurred with that style of music. This participant is speaking for many recovering addicts that may have administered heroin to a certain song and when they hear this song, romantic memories of the drug come to mind and the addiction is then triggered. The trigger that occurs in the mind of the recovering addict is creating a desire to use the heroin to recreate the comfort, and the indescribable feeling that the participants had mentioned earlier.

> In the beginning I did [missed the lifestyle]. In the beginning I would just think of it, would imagine pain and not feel it and I would just put my mind to something else, I stayed sober for six months, but I know I was tempted all the time. (Participant 6)

This addict has expressed that sobriety occurred for a short length of time and that through the six months of sobriety the thoughts of the lifestyle were clear in the recovering addict's mind. The sobriety ended after the six months because the addict was triggered and then used again. There are addicts that attempt recovery and are tempted easily and begin to reminisce about the "good times" and the relapse occurs creating a vicious cycle of addiction followed by treatment once again.

> Oh yes, totally, that is how it is now, I love the chaos um I'm addicted to the whole thing. Honestly, I liked going and buying a bunch of pills and selling them making some money and doing them myself. I lost money on some deals, but at least I made enough to get myself high. I miss picking up certain friends and going down to cop and for getting free bags and something. I miss going down to dope houses to sell. I miss walking around where I would get my drugs. Going to the houses of the people. There was one couple that I really care for but they do heroin and crack and you know I can't do that. I miss being over there with them. I miss it. I just miss the lifestyle, I miss being out all day and getting high all day. (Participant 10)

This participant is expressing that there is grief regarding the lifestyle and all its components. This participant is involved with treatment and continues to remember the exciting times of using heroin. here is grief involved with the addicts missing the people that were involved the constant contact with other addicts by using or by selling the heroin. While the participants were explaining the parts of the lifestyle that were missed, there was a sense of excitement and a sense of importance. The participants spoke of the lifestyle as if it were happening to them presently in the interview. These facial expressions and the continued conversation led me to believe that this lifestyle is important. The addict is grieving this part of his / her life that was bonding over a short or long period of time during the addiction. The participants in this study had the lifestyle visions were very vivid and the participants actually seemed to enjoy speaking about these memories and the people involved:

> It's not like we were really close friends. You know like the kind of friends you just joke around with and kind of light humor which is what I think everybody needs. Everybody else that I was still involved with were all serious stuff and sure we had a good time and we laughed and stuff, they loved me and they were concerned about me. These were people that were not concerned about my money or wondering if my pupils were dilated. It was easy friendship, they were acquaintances. (Participant 3)

This participant believes that the friendships that were formed in the lifestyle were important. The participant mentioned that the acquaintances loved her and that was important. Many heroin addicts develop friendships during their journey of addiction and these friendships hold high reverence for them as they recover. If the recovering addict attempts to restore or continue these friendships and all persons involved are not in recovery, the recovering addict will be tempted to relapse.

The lifestyle may be composed of relatives or very close friends. The recovery begins with the detachment from those individuals that are associated with heroin. This association does not exclude only other heroin addict, but includes suppliers too. Participant 11 shares the emotional tear of not being able to see a family member because there is a possibility of a relapse:

> My cousin sells drugs and I can no longer associate with him. That drives me crazy. He is highly supportive and he doesn't want to see me on drugs because he pedals drugs he knows that I have potential. I can't write him with a return address, just a hello.

The addict is not able to associate with any individual that is using heroin or selling heroin. The recovering addict has to go through this transformation to begin recovery and to continue sobriety. Recovering addicts begin to understand that there are certain crowds with whom they can't associate while in recovery. The addict disassociating himself / herself from the lifestyle and acquaintances can be traumatic, but becomes more devastating if there was ritual or a needle obsession prior to the recovery stage. The ritual and the needle obsession were of the utmost importance during the recovery period. The participants in this study were still dreaming of needles and thinking of rituals when recovery began even after there was some sobriety time involved.

Loss of Needle Obsession / Ritual

The participants in this study illustrated a strond bond with the needle. The participants included the use of the needle as part of the heroin ritual. The participants in this study discussed the use of the needle as if it were a separate but equal part of the heroin addiction. The participants in this study that used heroin intravenously had a fascination with the needle as well as the preparation of the needle to inject the heroin. It is important to note here that while the participants were describing the preparation of the needle and their fascination with it, the facial expressions could be defined as a person describing someone that they are highly infatuated with or possibly love. Participant 3 explains her fascination with the needle:

> Ritual. Well, I think us heroin addicts have this disease of addiction, but we have this needle obsession, watching everything go up the needle, watching the blood come up, everything about it is a fascination, it is really morbid, but every heroin addict that I have ever met that uses IV has the same thing.

This participant is stating that the needle obsession happens once the heroin addict begins recovery and there is not an opportunity to use the drug IV. The recovering addict begins to think about the use of the needle more leading to obsessing. This obsession could also be defined as an addiction to the needle. Participant 5 expresses her thoughts about the addiction to the needle:

> I think I'm addicted to the needle, I miss the ritual of going and copping and going over in the car and looking out – I guess just getting away with it. And then the needle the whole ritual, sticking the needle in my arm, I think I was just as addicted to the needle as I was to the heroin. I am still addicted to the needle.

She explained that, while in treatment, there is still an addiction to the needle. Unlike the addiction to the heroin, there is methadone to assist, however, with the needle obsession there is not another manner to rid this addiction. The recovering addict will then think about the needle and begin once again to reminisce about the needle and how it was used. This thought process could stimulate a relapse.

The recovering addict will think of the ritual of using the heroin and associated with the needle obsession. Participant 8 expresses his entire ritual and admits that he is missing this ritual while in treatment:

> I miss the part where I would get the powder of heroin, I would get the water mix it, I miss putting the part in my mouth and suck-up all the liquid, flip the needle getting all the air bubbles out registering it in the vein, watching the blood shooting through the syringe I miss putting the liquid in, I miss all that stuff.

The participants in this study were missing the ritual along with the needle just as much as they missed the heroin. The ritual included the use of the needle, but the second part of the ritual that the participants discussed was preparing the drug for administration. Obsessing over the needle during recovery, during treatment, or after treatment is definitely a relapse trigger for the recovering addict if the obsession continues. As participant 10 said, "I'm dreaming of needles. People are scared of needles, but I'm actually dreaming of sticking one in me, you know I was happy when the nurse came in and drew blood." This participant illustrates that the recovering addict will go to any lengths to feel the needle and that this can cause a recovery issue in the future once discharged from treatment. Participant 3 discussed how the needle obsession began in recovery:

> Just this morning I was looking at a girl here she was looking at her veins and she is a heroin addict too. I ruined my arms, I ruined this arm, this is not a burn, this is from shooting up too many times, having abscesses and they almost cut my arm off, I didn't care I wrapped it in bandages and continued using because there was a vein there. I don't know what is it going to take. What more can happen? (Participant 3)

The addicts that are attempting to recover have been distracted by the needle obsession. The needle obsession and the ritual of using affected the participants prior to treatment by the medical experience described by Participant 3. The needle obsession does not automatically go away according to the participants in this study and one can not escape the feeling especially if there are dreams about the needles. The participants in this study attempted to handle the needle obsession by waiting for the nurse to take blood. As described by participant 10, happiness was having the blood drawn.

Giving up the needle and the ritual of using heroin is a loss that the addict is grieving in treatment. The grief for the needle can be that the recovering addict simply misses the feeling of a prick in his / her vein. The grief of the ritual is that the addictive behavior such as going to obtain the heroin and preparing it is definitely a loss. One participant stated, "I prepare my utensils at the lunch table, in the same way I would prepare my works to use heroin." (Participant 4) This participant is referring to the instruments that are used when using heroin IV. The works include a needle, a spoon, a lighter, and a cotton ball along with something to force a vein to administer the drug. The needle obsession and the ritual is a hindrance in treatment unless it is addressed either in groups or during individual sessions.

Coping by Using Heroin

The participants in this study explained during the interview that heroin was always a reliable source during difficult times in life. The participants of this study mentioned that during their addiction if there was a loss the addict coped with the life event by using heroin. The participants explained that the heroin was used to numb the emotional pain that was being experienced. The participants also explained that during sobriety the urge to use heroin to cope with a loss or a traumatic experience was always present. The participants admitted that eventually they relapsed. The participants explained that the use did not occur immediately, but once the recovering addict relapsed he / she admitted that handling difficult situations seemed easier.

As mentioned earlier the heroin provides a comfort for the addict and also soothes the emotional or physical pain. As a result, the heroin has been used as a coping mechanism for a long period of time and has become a way of life for the addict. The participants in this study shared the ways that heroin assisted them in coping with experiences. Such experiences included grief either death or a traumatic experience. The participants also shared that they lacked coping skills and did not have a plan to cope until a negative situation presented itself.

Grief / Heroin as a means of coping

The participants in this study expressed that the heroin provided comfort especially during times of grief, in particular a death. The participants would use the heroin as a way to cope with the grief and the losses. Now that the addict has entered treatment he / she may reminisce the coping mechanisms used in the past. Participant 5 experience grief from feeling violated from a rape. This participant used the heroin to numb the feelings and the traumatic visions resulting from the rape:

> A rape that had happened when I was young, I don't think that I have actually ever spoke about it in a group, never ever the whole time in treatment. Well it is a destructive thing, because then I got a eating disorder then I started using heroin I see the one incident and where it has taken me to. I used to kill the pain from the rape. (Participant 5)

Participant 5 said that the rape was a violation and that heroin was used along with other addictions to heal the emotional pain caused by the rape. She is grieving and the heroin is a coping mechanism.

The participants in this study expressed that when they experienced grief such as a loss of family or a job, the use of heroin escalated. They used heroin to hide the emotional pain or the shame. For example Participant 6 states, "The last job I lost…there was freeze and I was part of that freeze so they had to lay me off and that just devastated me. I went down hill from that you know I used more." (Participant 6) This participant was grieving over the loss of employment and used heroin to grieve.

The heroin addicts that are in active addiction will use the heroin as a way to grieve as well as to escape. "It made me take a vacation mentally from what was happening. If I used heroin along with my Captain Morgan and Coke I guess I would be taking a mental break. Instead of having a mental break down, I was having a break with the drugs and the alcohol." (Participant 11) The participant compared the heroin as taking a mental break. The mental break is needed because the addict lacks the coping skills to handle the daily care of his terminally ill mother. The stressors of being a care taker and facing the death of a loved one becomes overwhelming for the participant and the heroin is used as a coping mechanism.

The participants in this study that have experienced death were very honest to say that the heroin assisted them to cope with the death of a loved one. "My mother passed away three months ago and I just ended up using again." (Participant 1) This participant used heroin as a coping mechanism to grieve his mother's death. He admitted that the use happened following the death. This is not uncommon that a heroin addict will relapse following the death of a close friend or relative. The heroin is used to provide comfort and to grieve the death.

Participant 3 expressed that she grieves her father's death on a daily basis and expressed how heroin was a coping mechanism during the death and thereafter:

> Yea, you know I grieve my father a lot. I really think that was the catalyst I am aware of it, but now I am out of control with it. I did grief counseling and stuff, but the drug helped relieve the pain at first because I was so depressed and sad.

Participant 3 was not able to handle her father's death and the participant used the heroin to relieve the sorrow and to attempt to alleviate symptoms of depression. Rather than trying to work at the group participation and process this participant fell back to coping by using heroin.

Participant 4 expressed that he was in sobriety and doing quite well, however, his infant child died and he returned to heroin to cope with the death and the grieving process: "I was working in a store and everything was going well and my baby died and then I relapsed." This participant illustrated that the lack of coping skills to handle grief can lead to a relapse during the sobriety period. The participant was sober, but the grief of the child's death was too much to handle so the participant used to receive the comfort and to grieve the death.

For some persons in recovery there may be a change in the family structure that leaves a void and can be traumatic for some recovering addicts. Participant 12 expresses how her son leaving the "nest" was traumatic for her. She dealt with the void of her son by using heroin she explains: "My son left and I felt so alone and sad – I used heroin to take away all that pain of my son leaving me alone – I can't take it." This participant had the grieving process of a child leaving the home. The participant admitted that the feeling of loneliness was overwhelming and the participant used the heroin to fill the void of the loneliness and the grief. It is important to note that during this part of the interview the participant was very tearful and appeared very sad when discussing this topic.

The use of heroin is a way that the addict handles grief. The addict uses to escape the feelings or to numb the emotions that accompany grief. The heroin provides a coping mechanism of comfort that enhances the relationship between the heroin addict and the drug. The addict that attends treatment attempts to end the relationship that stabilized during the grieving periods of the addict's life. The addict needs to cope with death, loneliness, and traumatic experiences without the use of heroin.

Lack of Coping Skills

The participants in this study expressed during the interview as well as when completing the questionnaire that they lacked coping skills. The recovering addicts lack the coping skills to handle difficult situations, boredom, living situations and recovery in general. The participants in this study were honest to state that they did not know how to cope. Through the evidence of the data the recovering addict used heroin to cope with everything in life, as a result, they are not lacking sober coping skills. The questions that were asked of the participants regarding coping in addiction and coping in sobriety seemed to be a struggle for them to discuss as fully as they did for the losses. The participants often stated that they used heroin to cope. As a result, new coping skills were not readily fresh to elaborate during our interview process.

Although Participant 2 expressed coping with situations better since he had support, there was some hesitation with coping well with the residential issues. He states, "I can handle the tough things because I have a good relationship with my fiancé and I am going to use my sponsor. Sometimes its real hard because I live in the same neighborhood." This participant has expressed a coping mechanism that will be helpful for him such as a sponsor and the support of his fiancé, there was a lack of confidence when coping with his environment.

The participants in this study expressed on different occasions that boredom played a vital role in their recent relapse. The participants of this study expressed that they did not have the correct coping mechanisms to handle boredom or to create activities during their recovery stage. This boredom is attributed to the chaotic lifestyle that the addict experienced before entering treatment and now that the lifestyle is not existent the recovering addict becomes bored. Participant 3 expresses her feelings about boredom: "No I get bored so easily, then I go back to visit my old using friends. It was the boredom and then I used." Participant 3 admits that when she is bored, she visits old friends that are in active addiction and this leads her to relapsing.

There were participants that were attending other treatment facilities for long- term treatment. Long - term treatment is approximately 90 – 120 days of treatment in a structured environment where more coping skills along with independent living skills are taught to the recovering addict. These participants illustrate that the recovering addicts in this study do not have a plan for coping. The recovering addicts will await a situation, and then react. Evidence of this data set illustrate that the addicts lack a plan and therefore lack coping skills. Participant 11 states how he intends on handling difficult situations in his future recovery:

> To be honest with you I am going to have to wait until a difficult situation comes along. I would think that I'm strong. I feel really strong this time. I have a bed waiting for me at another facility to get more time in. My family, I don't expect them to keep backing me. That's their life.

This participant was being very honest by stating he will wait for a situation. As this evidence shows that there was no plan of how he would handle difficult situations. There are recovering heroin addicts that do not prepare for a difficult situation and do not think through the difficulties that may appear. Participant 9 expressed that he did not know the coping mechanisms that he would use for difficult situations. He expressed:

> I am going to long term and I don't know how I am going to handle difficult situations. I guess I want to meditate or something, I would like to talk to someone and let it out or

something. I don't want to tell people things because I'm afraid that they will use it against me and it is like that with some people.

There are recovering addicts that admit that handling situations without the use of heroin is very difficult and they do not have an idea of how to handle such situations. The recovering addicts may keep the feelings to themselves and not discuss them.

The participants in this study constantly illustrated the struggle to handle situations without the use of heroin. Participant 7 expresses that he anticipants experiencing the urge to use while coping with various problems, however, he is stating that he will deal with the problem:

> Just regular coping skills, there are problems that I have to solve. You know problems are a part of life and people with problems are a part of life. Problems are gonna find me you know it's not like I'm going out there and have a great time. It's gonna be ahard. I'm gonna stress through job stress, through school stress and with everything that I do and be flipped – out of course, I'm gonna want to get high – but the whole thing I'm gonna think ok I'm gonna deal with it and you just do. (Participant 7)

There are some addicts that believe coping skills used for other addictions will be helpful when facing a serious situation. However, the recovering addict fails to recognize that coping skills from other addictions may not address the specific situation of the recovering heroin addict, which then creates a desire to use the drug.

Most participants in this study did not have coping mechanisms or plans to handle difficult situations without the use of heroin. The participants in this study expressed that they would wait until the difficult situation happened then think of a strategy. They have repeatedly used this plan, which leads to a failure in recovery. Participant 12 admits that she doesn't cope at all she just uses the heroin when she was in crisis.

> Participant 12 states, I'm so grateful to this place. I have to do my part, but I don't know how. I don't even cope I just say yea and use. I don't even think I just do it. I need a whole new brain. I can't see out of my right eye, I have dyslexia. I am slow and I have no education, I think I lost my turn.

This participant seems to have lost hope because she does not use or believes that she does not have coping skills to stay abstinent from heroin. This is a concern for the participant because she has other issues to contend with besides the urge to use heroin.

As one participant stated, recovery is up to the individual, the coping mechanisms are usually reviewed while in treatment; analyzing the data, the recovering heroin addict requires specific coping skills that is to focus on their urges and obsessions regarding the heroin. This next section focuses on some suggestions that the participants had for addressing the heroin problem in treatment.

Treatment is not addressing the problem

The participants in this study were involved in treatment more than once for a heroin relapse and expressed the reasons for the recent relapse. Most of the participants expressed that they do not do well after treatment. One reason is that they do not follow-through with treatment because the thought to use heroin is constantly on their minds. Participant 8 states:

> That is not how my frame of mind is right now. My mind frame is my disease I need constant reminders about the disease and all that to get this out of my head – I need someone to talk to all the time to get this out of my head.

This participant is expressing that sobriety is difficult because the heroin is constantly on his mind and this creates a problem in recovery. The participant is stating that he will need to discuss the constant thoughts about the heroin while in recovery, otherwise, there is a possibility for a relapse.

Some of the participants expressed that in the past they would use immediately following treatment. Although the reasons were mostly lack of coping skills and handling grief and losses there were two areas that participants wanted addressed in treatment prior to discharge. The two areas that may make a difference for recovery are: needle obsession and not discussing the feelings regarding missing the heroin.

Needle obsession

The participants in this study that discussed their obsession with the needle expressed that addressing the issue in treatment would be beneficial, Participant 3 states:

> I remember the first couple of weeks that I had clean, I started shooting coke, because I had to shoot something. It scared the hell out of me because I was saying oh I can shoot

coke now, cool; and nobody addresses that and I wondered why doesn't anybody address that.

This participant is concerned because the needle obsession has been experienced in the past led to a relapse. There is a serious concern that the groups are not addressing this obsession or the strategies that are needed to overcome this obsession. This obsession with the needle not only occurs during addiction, but also continues during recovery. This continued obsession appears to be a hindrance when the heroin addict is attempting to recover. The participants in this study recognized their needle obsession with themselves and with others. These participants discussed the obsession in grave detail, but didn't mention focusing on it in treatment. This was the only participant that actually stated that the needle obsession should be addressed while in treatment. She recognized that her obsession with the needle would lead to a relapse and she had a desire to change with the assistance of treatment.

Missing the heroin / Discussing feelings

The participants in this study were discussing their intense relationship with heroin and at times mentioned that if the heroin were in front of them the recovering addict would not be able to say no. Missing the heroin is accompanied with the characteristics of the relationship and the participants in this study appeared to need more discussion on their emotional ties to the heroin and its effects. Participant 4 expresses during this interview that he has relapsed in the past because he has not discussed the feelings he misses about heroin. He mentioned earlier that he enjoys the relaxed feeling and how heroin helps him to forget about everything. This participant however does not get an opportunity to express these feelings in group and as a result he has relapsed in the past. This participant is expressing how the groups can be improved to help him in his recovery:

> It's hard to find it here, the groups are weak, they focus on the wrong things, they got their mind on the wrong things. You gotta have groups in a circle that people can talk and let out their feelings – and get to know each other and give you what you are looking for, it is to survive.

The participant is expressing that the topics of the group need to address the specific issues of the recovering heroin addict. The need to discuss the feelings and emotions regarding the heroin is important for the recovery to begin in the treatment facility.

Some of the participants in this study recognized that treatment was a positive place to begin recovery. Some participants were able to recognize through the groups that they had become a different person because of the lifestyle and the culture of heroin addiction. The data presents itself that the participants were feeling safe and confident while in treatment, but had difficulty when returning to his / her environment to begin the recovery process.

Self-Help Groups

Participant 3 expressed that during groups mainly self-help groups there was a sense of security and high self-esteem, however, these feelings did not last once she was left alone:

> Well in group you have a lot of confidence, it raises your self esteem, it really does. However, when you are back by yourself you know I am thinking it is me again. You start thing about getting high, you have $30.00 bucks in your purse and you say come on let's get high.

The recovering addict has strong belief in sobriety during a group, but has difficulty transferring the belief once alone. There are recovering addicts who do well in the confinement of the rehabilitation unit, but have difficulty with sobriety once in his / her environment. This participant was able to recognize that there was a consistent problem after she left group and that her self – esteem was elevated only in the group session and decreased when alone.

Along with the feeling of confidence, there is also a feeling of serenity as described by Participant 2. This feeling of peace and tranquility may be an avenue used for some recovering addicts to continue sobriety, but not for others. The feeling of tranquility for this participant was only in treatment, once he returned to his neighborhood the feeling of peace soon disappeared.

Participant 10 utilized the self-help groups to recognize that she was a different person since using heroin. The groups used as a tool for her to attempt to make a change, she states: "I'm thinking of the type of person I've turned into. I don't want to be like that." This participant had begun to realize that her character had changed since using heroin. This participant did not elaborate any further if any activities where planned to work on her character change while in sobriety.

Participant 7, however, did not choose to comment on the groups or anything in treatment he felt that he did not need treatment to address his problem just depending on his past experience he states:

> I don't think so. I think the only thing that makes me know that I'm not doing these drugs again is myself – that's the only person that is gonna do it. I'm gonna try not to forget that pills messed me up you know what I mean.

This participant is stating that he will need to believe in the inner strength to not use the opiate. He is stating that remembering the effect of the drug will assist him to not use the opiate. This participant is depending only on himself and not on the skills taught during groups.

Also, participant 8 also did not have anything in treatment that was convincing to discontinue use, nor did he comment on the groups; but the participant admitted that there is a desire to stop because of the "never ending cycle." "It's just that I'm just sick of going through the same s___ over and over for the past four years – it's just a never ending cycle…It's like I know everything I am just not applying it." This participant is stating that although he knows everything, he continues to use the heroin. The participant, however, states that he was exhausted from using the heroin and attempting recovery over the past four years.

Although, there were the participants that chose not to comment on the groups, participant 6 observed groups from a different point of view. He describes the groups as positive which coincides with participant 3 who stated that the groups increase her self-esteem. Participant 6 also expressed the topics that he learned from the self-help groups while in treatment, he states: "Oh yes, positives, I need positive thinking that is what I need. I got a lot of information to control your urges and how to overcome obstacles and that is what I've got to overcome, my environment, people, places and things, that is what I've got to do."

This participant discussed the topics that he needs to continue working on after treatment is complete when he returns to his environment. He also expressed the information given on controlling urges, but did not specify if it were for recovering heroin addicts or substance abusers in general.

The participants in this study gave information regarding the path that treatment has taken them in the past, as well as where they would like treatment in the future. The participants in this study expressed the reasons that relapsed occurred in the past and considered the different topics that could be addressed in treatment to address the problem of heroin relapse.

Summary

The overall theme of **Ending the heroin relationship** consists of the recovering addict addressing the losses that accompany the addiction: *loss of heroin, loss of culture, loss of lifestyle, loss of drug family (acquaintances), loss of comfort, loss of needle and loss of ritual and learning to cope without heroin.* The theory is that the recovering addict needs to address these areas while in treatment to eliminate unresolved and disenfranchised grief. The groups that are formed need to be specifically for the heroin addict. These areas can be addressed in groups or individual sessions to benefit the recovering heroin addict. When the treatment facilities do not address these issues the recovering heroin addict grieves silently and the results are disenfranchised grief and ultimately relapse.

CHAPTER V
DISCUSSION

This fifth chapter will provide a discussion of the results presented in this study surrounding the main theme and the theory that emerged from the data. This chapter will also include implications and limitations of the study along with an area of further research and recommendations.

The main theme that emerged from the data was **Ending the relationship with heroin.** The theory of this study: **Individuals that are attempting recovery grieve the loss of heroin and its components. If these losses are not addressed, unresolved and disenfranchised grief results increasing the likelihood of relapse.**

Ways of Coping Questionnaire

The Ways of Coping Questionnaire was used to stimulate the participant's thoughts prior to the interview and was a useful tool for the participants to recognize if their coping skills were sufficient or insufficient. The participants in this study overall agreed that they lacked coping skills and had difficulty sustaining sobriety once discharged from a treatment facility. The Ways of Coping Questionnaire (Folkman & Lazarus, 1988) was ranked according to the coping styles of the general population that were: 1. confrontive coping, 2. distancing, 3. self – controlling, 4. seeking social support, 5. accepting responsibility, 6. escape – avoidance, 7. planful problem solving, and 8. positive reappraisal. The ranking for this study was: 1. accepting responsibility, 2. confrontive coping, 3. self-controlling, 4. escape-avoidance, 5. seeking social support, 6. distancing, 7. planful problem solving and 8. positive reappraisal.

The scales that had a major difference in ranking between the two populations were distancing and accepting responsibility. The participants of this study appeared to take responsibility for their role in a problem that they had in the past. The participants in this study also used distancing less than the general population. They detach themselves from the problem nor did they minimize the problem.

Interview Results

The main theme that emerged from the data was ending the relationship with the heroin. The theory resulting from this theme is that individuals addicted to heroin grieve the loss of the drug and the drug culture; if these losses are not addressed the results are unresolved and disenfranchised grief. The unresolved and disenfranchised creates difficulty because the addicts are not able free themselves from the grips of the drug and its culture and lack coping skills to resolve these losses. As a result, ending the relationship with the heroin is crucial for the recovery process to begin, the recovering addict must grieve the loss of the heroin and all the losses associated with the drug. The losses associated with the drug are the heroin lifestyle and the heroin culture. The lifestyle of the heroin addict includes the methods used to obtain and maintain the addiction. The heroin culture is the socialization that is associated with the group of people that share the same common factor, the heroin.

According to Kaczkowski and Zygmond (1991) substance abusers grieve the loss of friends, significant others, and alcohol. Also according to Beecham, Prewitt and Scholar (1996) the substance abusers grieved the loss of self – respect, loss of freedom of choice(s), loss of confidence in others, loss of self-trust, loss of self-confidence and the loss of respect from others. The participants in this study seldom mentioned that while they felt hurt that there was a loss of family or of material things; they primarily grieved the loss of heroin along with the lifestyle and the culture. The anguish from the detachment of heroin causes the most grief during treatment and continues in recovery as unresolved grief. The recovering addicts in this study had a difficult time separating from the drug because of losing the benefits of the drug and all its components. Importantly, because these losses were not recognized or addressed in treatment, they resulted in unresolved grief. The failure of the treatment to address the unresolved grief from the losses related to heroin addiction, lifestyle and culture may be one of the factors that often leads to relapse.

Further, the participants in the study were clear that losing heroin was similar to losing a best friend or a lover. They often described the use of the heroin as a form of comfort that was a coping mechanism during turmoil in their lives. One of the participants compared the attachment / comfort to “being in the arms of an angel.” Heroin represents security, assurance, and self – confidence which most of the addicts did not have unless they used. The loss of the euphoric feeling and thoughts about how to regain it were a constant struggle for the recovering addicts in this study. This struggle represents the unresolved grief regarding the losses related to the heroin and the recovering addict not being ready to let go of the heroin or its counterparts because he / she has not gone through the process of grieving the drug.

An example of participants in this study that were not ready to detach from the drug are those that admitted if there was a possibility of using heroin without negative consequences they would use for a lifetime. These participants were disappointed in themselves at not being able to separate from the drug nor from the anticipation of the euphoric relaxed feeling that heroin produced. The participants discussed that they were "in love" or "hooked" on the feeling and that therapists / clinicians should recognize that these feelings are important and need to be addressed using a non-judgmental approach in treatment.

Another finding related to disenfranchised grief and treatment issues is the ritual and obsession of the needle use. The needle obsession developed during heroin use, but continued in recovery. This obsession was presented in the form of dreams of use during recovery and that the addict yearns to have an encounter with a needle, which included blood draws while in treatment. The recovering addicts that used heroin IV spoke of the needle with such fascination, infatuation, and with such detail that the separation was obviously painful. The needle obsession appeared to haunt the participants during their recovery and impeded the healing process. The loss of the heroin and the loss of the needle appeared to be a very emotional topic for the participants and these two losses seemed to contribute to chronic relapses. The recovering addicts admitted that they missed the daily ritual and had difficulty detaching. The ritual includes the daily use of the heroin along with the preparation to administer the drug via IV, nasal, oral or skin-popping.

During the interviews the participants were asked what caused the recent relapse and most indicated that a difficult situation presented itself and heroin was used as a coping mechanism. The participants were dealing with stress from family, the death of a loved one, or a significant loss and heroin was a way of coping (Walter, 1994; Blume & Schmaling, 1996; Ojesjo, 2000). The recovering addicts relapsed because they had not ended the relationship with heroin and still depended on it for comfort.

The treatment facilities over the years have focused on balancing the lifestyle from addiction to recovery by changing people / places / and things to prevent a relapse once discharged from a treatment facility (Marlatt & Gordon, 1985). Most recovering heroin addicts are unable to change their living environment, because the lack the financial resources to relocate. As a result, the recovering addict has not fully grieved the losses related to heroin and faces the same environment after treatment accompanied by the unresolved grief issues the unable to cope except via the drug, resulting in relapse.

In conclusion the results of these interviews illustrated very clearly that the recovering addicts in treatment are experiencing losses of the heroin, lifestyle and culture. The treatment providers are not addressing these three major losses and their intricacies resulting in disenfranchised grief. The way the recovering addicts discussed their drug, with such love and admiration it is evident that the recovering addicts in treatment have not been given the opportunity to grieve heroin or the losses related to its use. The recovering addicts in this study have not been processing the grief during treatment, which makes it harder to end the relationship with heroin and therefore leaves a door open to relapse. The participants in this study cognitively struggled with knowing recovery was vital, but the desire to continue using at times was overpowering because of the deep attachment issues. This struggle identified in the data exemplifies the need for losses directly related to the heroin addiction to be addressed in treatment and process the grief by developing coping skills with the recovering addicts prior to discharge.

Limitations of the study

First, this study was designed for one scheduled interview during the detoxification stage at the treatment facility. It may have been beneficial if the participants were interviewed a second time toward the end of their 28-day stay to identify their grief status with the losses the recovering addicts pointed out in the interviews. Unfortunately, because of the treatment facility closing and the lack of accessibility to heroin addicts in the rehabilitation status, a second interview was not possible. Second, the need for one or two open – ended questions focusing on coping skills specifically for the heroin addict while in treatment would have been useful for strengthening the this study.

Conclusions and Implications of the study

This study found that the recovering addicts grieve the loss of heroin in three aspects: the drug itself, the lifestyle, and the culture. This study revealed that the heroin addict mourns the loss of the drug and its counterparts in a more heartfelt way than primary relationships prior to addiction. The therapists / clinicians that are working with the heroin population need to understand the importance of addressing the losses and their impact on recovery. The recovering addict requires a therapist / clinician to listen holistically, taking in consideration all losses, but focusing on the losses that are germane to heroin addiction that may cause problems in recovery. The therapist / clinician that processes the losses by allowing the recovering addict to grieve the drug, the lifestyle, and the culture is decreasing disenfranchised grief and increasing an opportunity for recovery.

Recommendations

This study found that recovering heroin addicts in detoxification grieve the loss of the heroin, the lifestyle and the culture and lacked the coping skills to deal with these losses while in treatment or after treatment. The recovering addicts specifically were grieving the heroin as they would grieve the loss of a friend and were painfully grieving the absence of the needle. As a result of these findings, it is recommended that during treatment therapists / clinicians help the recovering addicts process the grief from these losses and help create coping skills to better manage these losses once discharged.

Future Research

The first needed area of research is for the recovering addicts to have a follow-up study after detoxification for approximately one year to monitor the recovery as well as to monitor the resolution of the losses. The second area of research is for therapists / clinicians to report in either a qualitative or quantitative research design how they are providing treatment interventions for the losses from heroin addiction to decrease disenfranchised grief.

Overall, further research in the area of unresolved grief related to heroin addiction is necessary to develop treatment modalities that eliminate disenfranchised grief and expand the treatment modalities to address the specific needs of the recovering heroin addict.

References

Bammer, G., & Weekes, S. (1994). Becoming an ex-user: Insights into the process and implications for treatment and policy. *Drug and Alcohol Review, 13,* 285-292.

Beechem, M. H.; Prewitt, J. & Scholar, J. (1996). Loss – grief addiction model. *Journal of Drug Education 26(2)*, 183-198.

Blume, A., & Schmaling, K. B. (1996). Loss and readiness to change substance abuse. *Addictive Behaviors, 21(4)*, 527-530.

Bowlby, J. (1969). Attachment and loss. New York: Basic Books.

Bowlby, J. (1980). Attachment and loss volume 1. New York: Viking Pegiun.

Bowlby, J. (1982). Attachment and loss: Second Edition. London: Institute of Psycho-Analysis.

Dai, J. & Zhao, Z. (2001). Mental health status of the first – degree relatives of heroin dependent patients. *Chinese Journal of Clinical Psychology, 9(2),* 148-152.

Doka, K. J. (1989). Disenfranchised grief: Recognized hidden sorrow. Lexington Books: Massachusetts/Toronto.

Engle, G. (1964, September). Grief and grieving. *American Journal of Nursing, 64(9)*, 93-98.

Francis, D.; Kaiser, D., & Deaver, S. P. (2003). Representations of attachment security in the bird's nest drawings of clients with substance abuse disorders. *Art Therapy: Journal of the American Art Therapy Association, 20(3),* 126-137.

Folkman, S., & Lazarus, R. S. (1988). Mind Garden, Consulting Psychologists Press, Inc.

Frontline PBS Documentary on "The Opium Kings" www.pbs.org

Glaser, B. (1978). Theoretical sensitivity. Mill Valley, CA: Sociology Press.

Gossop, M.; Stewart, D.; Browne, N.,& Marsden, J. (2002). Factors associated with abstinence, lapse or relapse to heroin use after residential treatment: protective effect of coping responses. *Society for the Study of Addiction to Alcohol and Other Drugs, 97,* 1259-1267.

Hazen, M. A., (2003). Societal and workplace responses to perinatal loss: Disenfranchised grief or healing connection. *Human Relations, 56 (2),* 147-166.

Helmlinger, T. (1977). After you've said goodbye: how to recover after ending a relationship. New York: Schenkman Publishing Company.

Howard, T. (2003). Heroin. San Diego, California: Lucent Books.

Huang, H; Wu, X; Lin, M; Wen, D, & Zheng, C. (2001). An investigation on the mental health of Heroin addicts. *Chinese Journal of Clinical Psychology, 9(1)*, 58-59.

Khantzian, E. J.; Mack, J. E. & Schatzberg, A. F. (1974). Heroin use as an attempt to cope: clinical obserservations.

Kosten, T. R.; Rounsaville, B. J., & Kleber, H. D. (1983). Relationship of depression to Psychosocial stressors in heroin addicts. *Journal of Nervous and Mental Disease, 17(2),* 97-104.

Kubler – Ross (1969). On death and dying. New York: Macmillan.

Kaczkowski, V.R. & Zygmond, M.J. (1992). Grief resolution in the recovery of individuals who are addicted to alcohol. *Journal of Mental Health Counseling 13(3),* 356-366.

Krueger, D. W. (1981). Stressful life events and the return to heroin use. *Journal of Human Stress, 7(2),* 3-8.

Lindemann, E. (1944). Symptomatology and management of acute grief. *American Journal of Psychiatry, 101*, 141-148.

Marlatt, G. A. & Gordon, J. R. (1985). Relapse prevention: maintenance strategies in the treatment of addictive behaviors. New York: The Guilford Press.

McDonald, P. C., 1985. Grieving a healing process. Hazelden Foundation.

McGovern, T. (1986). Loss identification in the treatment of alcoholism. *Alcohol 3*, 95-96.

McGovern, T. (1986). The effects of comprehensive inpatient alcoholism treatment on measures of loss and grief. *Alcohol, 3,* 89-92.

Merrill, J.; Alterman, A., & Cacciola, J., Rutherford, M. (1999). Prior treatment history and its impact on criminal recidivism. *Journal of Substance Abuse Treatment, 17(4),* 313-319.

Ojesjo, L. (2000). The recovery from alcohol problems over the life course: The Lundby longitudinal study, Sweden. *Alcohol, 22*, 1-5.

Platt, J. J. (1986). Heroin addiction: Theory, research, and treatment; Second Edition. Malabar, Fla: R.E. Krieger Publishing Company.

Platt, J. J. (1995). Heroin addiction: Theory, research, and treatment, Volume 2 The addict, the treatment process and social control. Malabar, Fla: R.E. Krieger Publishing Company.

Rando, T. (1988). Grieving: How to go on living when someone you love dies.

Lexington, Massachusetts: Lexington Books.

Roback, & Weitzman (1994-1995)

Schuster, C. R. & Kuhar, M. J. (Ed.) (1996). Pharmacological aspects of drug dependence: Toward an integrated neurobehavioral approach. New York: Springer.

Strauss, A., & Corbin, J. (1998). Basics of qualitative research: Grounded theory procedures and techniques. Newbury Park, CA: Sage Publications.

Sroufe, L. A. (1996). Emotional development: the organization of emotional life in the early years. New York: Cambridge University Press.

Tiebout, H. M. (1949). The act of surrender in the therapeutic process: With special reference to alcoholism. *Quarterly Journal of Studies on Alcohol, 10*, 48-58.

United States Department of Health and Human Services: Substance Abuse and Mental Health Services Administration Center for Substance Abuse Prevention www.samhsa.gov.

United States Department of Health and Human Services: Substance Abuse and Mental Health Services Administration Center for Substance Abuse Prevention Treatment Episode Data Set (TEDS) (May 2004) www.samhsa.gov.

Walters, G. (1994). The drug lifestyle: One pattern or several? *Psychology of Addictive Behaviors, 8(1),* 8-13.

Worden, J. W. (1982). Grief counseling and grief therapy: A handbook for the mental health professional. New York: Springer Publishing Co.

Worden, J. W. (2002). Grief counseling and grief therapy: A handbook for the mental health practitioner. Third Edition. New York: Springer Publishing Co.

Appendix A

Recruitment Script

The PI will state the recruitment script:

Hello my name is Davina Moss and I am conducting a research project entitled "Unresolved grief and loss issues related to substance abuse." The project is focusing on grief / losses during heroin addiction or during recover period from heroin and the manner in which you had coped with these situations. This information will be obtained from at most two audio taped interviews that I will conduct with you in a private room located in the hospital. The first part of the interview will consist of you completing the Ways of Coping Questionnaire by Folkman and Lazarus (1988), which will give you and I an indication of how you have coped with difficult situations. We will then proceed with four phases of interview questions about your addiction that will be audio taped. The audiotape will not have any identifying information and will be kept confidential unless there is a known risk of harming yourself or someone else. The second interview will discuss any unfinished business from the first interview or other issues that were pertinent to the topic. If you have any questions regarding the topic or the project I have paper and envelopes that can be sealed at the receptionist's desk for you to write notes and leave in my mailbox as needed.

In the event that you are suffering from any emotional distress during the interview you are allowed to discontinue the interview at anytime with no penalty. If you have feelings of doing harm to yourself or someone else, please inform me immediately. I will refer you to the treatment team leader for appropriate assistance and or assessments. Thank you for your time and your participation in this study.

Appendix B

Questions for the Project will be in four phases:

Phase One:

1. Prior to your addiction did you suffer any losses?
2. How did you cope with these losses prior to addiction?
3. What was the parental influence on loss and coping mechanisms?

Phase Two:

1. During your addiction did you suffer any losses?
2. How did you cope with these losses?

Phase Three:

1. During your sobriety period did you suffer any losses?
2. What were your coping mechanisms?
3. During your sobriety period did you feel loss for the lifestyle of addiction?

3a. What do you miss about the lifestyle?

3b. Do you miss any of the acquaintances from addiction?

3c. Do you feel a loss now that heroin is not in your life?

3d. What do you plan to do about the loss of heroin?

4. When sober / clean did you miss anything from your addiction?

Phase Four:

1. What caused your recent relapse?
2. Is there anything that has happened in rehab that makes you know that you will not use again?
3. Are you prepared to handle difficult situations without the use of heroin?
4. Do you think that sobriety will be a natural progression for you?

Debriefing Questions (Used after each interview)

1. How are you feeling after this interview?
2. Is there anything that you mentioned in an earlier answer that you wanted to discuss in further detail?
3. Is there any part of the interview that was distressing or made you very uncomfortable?

4. Do you feel that you will hurt yourself or someone else after we have completed this interview?

Appendix C

Unresolved Grief and Loss Issues Related to Substance Abuse Study

Demographics

Interview # _____

Name: _________________________ Code: _______

Address: ____

City: _____________________

State: _____________________ Zip Code: _________

Married: ___ YES ___ NO

Age: ______

Race: ___ African American; ___ Asian; ___ Hispanic; ___ Native American; __ White

Age of first use: ______ Substance Used first: _______________

Age of first use for heroin: _____

Method of use: __ IM __ IV __ Nasal __ Skin 'popping'

Please provide the following information:

Name: OMIT Date: ____________
Month / Day / Year

Identification Number (optional): ____________ Gender (Circle): **M** F Age: ____

Marital Status (check): ❑ Single ❑ Married ❑ Widowed ❑ Separate/Divorced

TO THE COUNSELOR

Fill out your Institutional Address below:

OMIT

Name/ Institution:

OMIT

Address

Instructions

To respond to the statements in this questionnaire, you must have a specific stressful situation in mind. Take a few moments and think about the most stressful situation that you have experienced in the *past week*.

By "stressful" we mean a situation that was difficult or troubling for you, either because you felt distressed about what happened, or because you had to use considerable effort to deal with the situation. The situation may have involved your family, your job, your friends, or something else important to you. Before responding to the statements, think about the details of this stressful situation, such as where it happened, who was involved, how you acted, and why it was important to you. While you may still be involved in the situation, or it could have already happened, it should be the most stressful situation that you experienced during the week.

As you respond to each of the statements, please keep this stressful situation in mind. **Read each statement carefully and indicate, by circling 0, 1, 2 or 3 , to what extent you used it in the situation.**

Key: 0 = Does not apply or not used 1 = Used somewhat
2 = Used quite a bit 3 = Used a great deal

Please try to respond to every question.

0 = Does not apply or not used	1 = Used somewhat	2 = Used quite a bit	3 = Used a great deal

1. I just concentrated on what I had to do next – the next step. 0 1 2 3
2. I tried to analyze the problem in order to understand it better. 0 1 2 3
3. I turned to work or another activity to take my mind off things. 0 1 2 3
4. I felt that time would have made a difference – the only thing was to wait. 0 1 2 3
5. I bargained or compromised to get something positive from the situation. 0 1 2 3
6. I did something that I didn't think would work, but at least I was doing something. 0 1 2 3
7. I tried to get the person responsible to change his or her mind. 0 1 2 3
8. I talked to someone to find out more about the situation. 0 1 2 3
9. I criticized or lectured myself. 0 1 2 3
10. I tried not to burn my bridges, but leave things open somewhat. 0 1 2 3
11. I hoped for a miracle. 0 1 2 3
12. I went along with fate; sometimes I just have bad luck. 0 1 2 3
13. I went on as if nothing had happened. 0 1 2 3
14. I tried to keep my feelings to myself. 0 1 2 3
15. I looked for the silver lining, so to speak; I tried to look on the bright side of things. 0 1 2 3
16. I slept more than usual. 0 1 2 3
17. I expressed anger to the person(s) who caused the problem. 0 1 2 3
18. I accepted sympathy and understanding from someone. 0 1 2 3
19. I told myself things that helped me feel better. 0 1 2 3
20. I was inspired to do something creative about the problem. 0 1 2 3
21. I tried to forget the whole thing. 0 1 2 3
22. I got professional help. 0 1 2 3

Go on to next page

0 = Does not apply or not used 1 = Used somewhat 2 = Used quite a bit 3 = Used a great deal

23. I changed or grew as a person.	0	1	2	3
24. I waited to see what would happen before doing anything.	0	1	2	3
25. I apologized or did something to make up.	0	1	2	3
26. I made a plan of action and followed it.	0	1	2	3
27. I accepted the next best thing to what I wanted.	0	1	2	3
28. I let my feelings out somehow.	0	1	2	3
29. I realized that I had brought the problem on myself.	0	1	2	3
30. I came out of the experience better than when I went in.	0	1	2	3
31. I talked to someone who could do something concrete about the problem.	0	1	2	3
32. I tried to get away from it for a while by resting or taking a vacation.	0	1	2	3
33. I tried to make myself feel better by eating, drinking, smoking, using drugs, or medications, etc.	0	1	2	3
34. I took a big chance or did something very risky to solve the problem.	0	1	2	3
35. I tried not to act too hastily or follow my first hunch.	0	1	2	3
36. I found new faith.	0	1	2	3
37. I maintained my pride and kept a stiff upper lip.	0	1	2	3
38. I rediscovered what is important in life.	0	1	2	3
39. I changed something so things would turn out all right.	0	1	2	3
40. I generally avoided being with people.	0	1	2	3
41. I didn't let it get to me; I refused to think too much about it.	0	1	2	3
42. I asked advice from a relative or friend I respected.	0	1	2	3
43. I kept others from knowing how bad things were.	0	1	2	3
44. I made light of the situation; I refused to get too serious about it.	0	1	2	3

Go on to next page

0 = Does not apply or not used   1 = Used somewhat   2 = Used quite a bit   3 = Used a great deal

45. I talked to someone about how I was feeling. 0 1 2 3

46. I stood my ground and fought for what I wanted. 0 1 2 3

47. I took it out on other people. 0 1 2 3

48. I drew on my past experiences; I was in a similar situation before. .. 0 1 2 3

49. I knew what had to be done, so I doubled my efforts to make things work. 0 1 2 3

50. I refused to believe that it had happened. 0 1 2 3

51. I promised myself that things would be different next time. 0 1 2 3

52. I came up with a couple of different solutions to the problem. 0 1 2 3

53. I accepted the situation, since nothing could be done. 0 1 2 3

54. I tried to keep my feeling about the problem from interfering with other things. 0 1 2 3

55. I wished that I could change what had happened or how I felt. 0 1 2 3

56. I changed something about myself. 0 1 2 3

57. I daydreamed or imagined a better time or place than the one I was in. 0 1 2 3

58. I wished that the situation would go away or somehow be over with. 0 1 2 3

59. I had fantasies or wishes about how things might turn out. 0 1 2 3

60. I prayed. 0 1 2 3

61. I prepared myself for the worst. 0 1 2 3

62. I went over in my mind what I would say or do. 0 1 2 3

63. I thought about how a person I admire would handle this situation and used that as a model. 0 1 2 3

64 I tried to see things from the other person's point of view. 0 1 2 3

65. I reminded myself how much worse things could be. 0 1 2 3

66. I jogged or exercised. 0 1 2 3

Stop Here.

Appendix D

Category 2

Losses

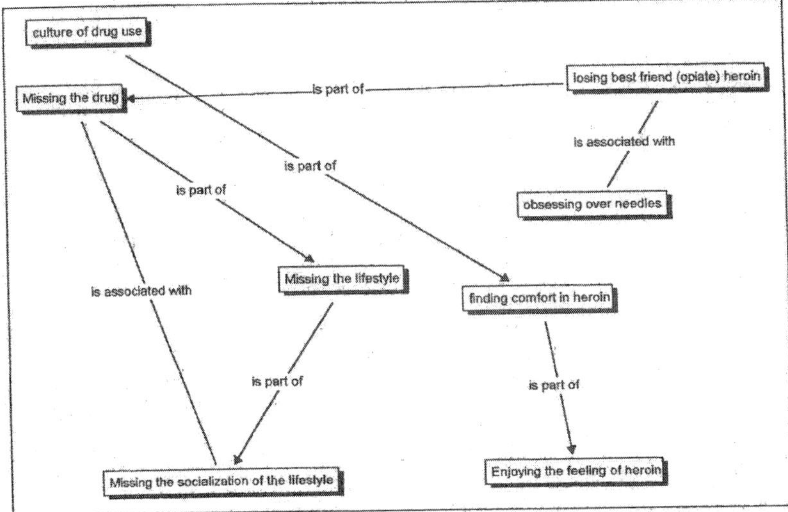

Category 3

Choice to cope by using heroin

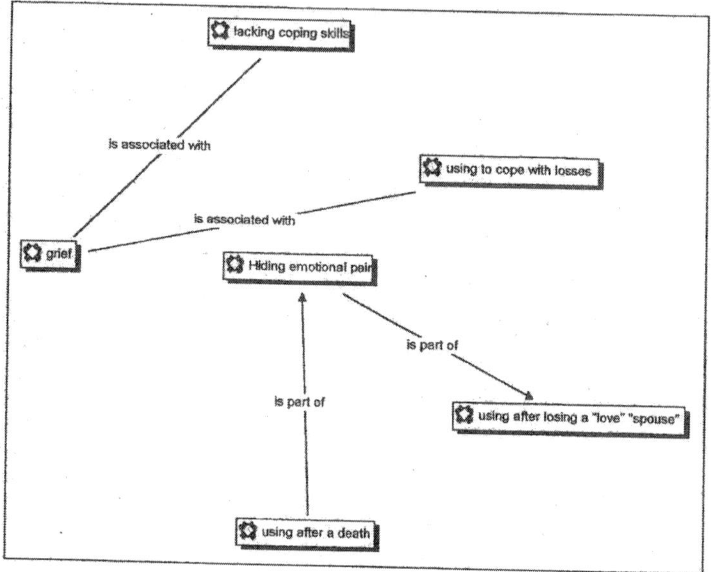

Category 4

Treatment is not addressing the problem

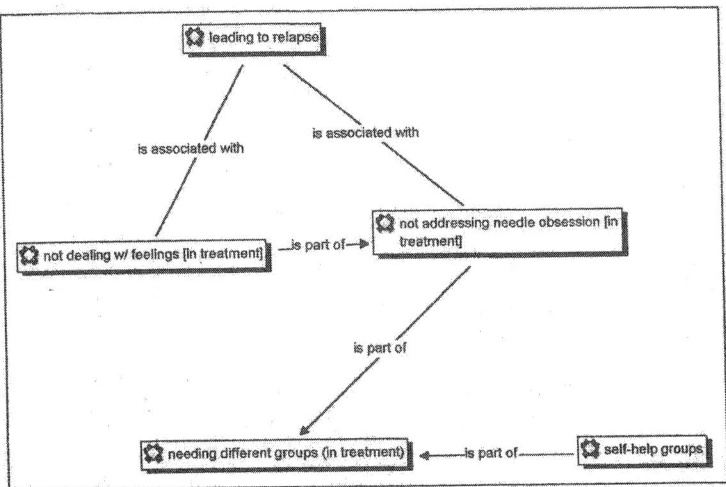

Made in the USA
Middletown, DE
23 May 2015